# Royal Postcards

Jack H. Smith

*On the Cover: clockwise from top:*

The children of Russia's tsar: lives tragically abbreviated. Rotary. R3, **$15.**

Queen Victoria of Spain and daughter. Queen "Ena" was the sweetheart of the Spanish people but was ill-treated by her husband. Rotary. R2, **$10.**

Grande Duchesse Charlotte of Luxembourg with her husband. Charlotte reigned from 1919 to 1964. She died in 1985 just short of her ninetieth birthday. R4, **$20.**

George V of England and family. Philco. R2, **$10.**

Heir to the throne of Austria-Hungary, Franz Ferdinand with his morganatic wife, Sophie Chotek. R4, **$20.**

Cecilie, the German Crown-Princess. N.P.G. R2, **$10.**

*Center:*

German Emperor Wilhelm II. Clothing to match an outsized ego. R2, **$10.**

To my wife, Sherry and our daughter, Shanna, this book is gratefully dedicated.

Special thanks for the encouragement of Gary Hauge and Marilyn Tataryn.

*Cover design: Ann Eastburn*
*Interior layout: Anthony Jacobson*

*ISBN 0-87069-495-2*

*Library of Congress Catalog Card number 87-050014*

*Copyright © 1987*
*Jack H. Smith*

*10 9 8 7 6 5 4 3 2 1*

*Published by*

**Wallace-Homestead**
publishers of fine books

*Wallace-Homestead Book Company*
*580 Waters Edge*
*Lombard, Illinois 60148*

*One of the ABC PUBLISHING Companies*

# Contents

# Acknowledgments

For the assistance of His Imperial Majesty Archduke Otto von Habsburg-Lorraine, I shall be forever grateful. That a man of His Majesty's stature and manifold responsibilities would willingly find the time to aid me in my research fills me with an endless sense of appreciation.

Special gratitude is also extended to William F. Huber, friend, teacher, and fellow historian. Bill and I spent countless hours discussing many of the royal personages illustrated herein and, for periods all too brief, managed to breathe life once more into their deeds and characters.

Finally, and most importantly, I wish to acknowledge my appreciation to God. Without my faith in Him as a guiding light, I would consider any and all activities as equally meaningless.

# Preface

The current spate of books that have royalty as their central theme reveals a new preoccupation with a form of government that remains as an anachronism in the twentieth century. Previously relegated to the sterile pages of dust-covered history texts, yesterday's autocrats had slipped quietly into academic obscurity. Unmolested by attention, seemingly forgotten, and certainly unneeded by men who cherish democratic ideals above all else, memories of them existed primarily in the minds of historians.

Then, sometime in the 1960s and 1970s, an interest in the vanishing royal breed started to emerge. Like the mythical phoenix rising from the ashes of its former glory, the mystery and aura that has always surrounded kingship began to enthrall the imagination of a new generation. And, because royal personages could now be studied and examined from the safety that time and distance afforded, their pomp and arrogance might be graciously redefined as majesty and imperial whim.

Several incidents, all involving their modern counterparts, may be cited for this revived interest; the deposing of monarchies in Greece and Iran, the recrowning of a Spanish king, and the installation of new rulers in Holland and Luxembourg. Feeding the movement in the 1980s has been the attention focused on the marriage of Prince Charles, the next king of England, and the birth of his first son.

The many period mementos and items of memorabilia have also served as instruments to sustain the spell of attraction. Medals, coins, stamps, souvenir spoons, commemorative plates, and all sorts of paper ephemera are being encountered today with increasing frequency. Among the last identified group, the one with which this volume is concerned, is that ubiquitous revealer of all things human, the picture postcard. The few remaining royal houses, being beneficiaries of the interest upsurge, have not been forgotten, and cards of them may be found in relative abundance.

But, it is the former rulers with their more pretentious life-styles and less restricted use of power who seem to be the most attractively romantic figures. Once again, the postcard has not neglected its duty. For, while the record is far from being complete, the postcard has been amazingly inclusive. Not only are their highnesses depicted in traditional splendor, resting their regal bodies atop satin cushions, but the collector and purveyor is also allowed to view the monarch engaging in all sorts of activities, both those related to their royal position and those more mundane in nature.

Such a series of portraits is of obvious value to collector and historian alike. Moreover, some specimens are of considerable worth. It is hoped that readers previously unaware of these royal photographic and artistic renderings will do more than simply pause and gaze but that they may be encouraged to become participants in a collecting field with an appeal that is truly universal.

# Introduction

In this age of instant, sometimes shallow analysis, few institutions have escaped criticism. Many of them seem to have an abiding fear of sharing the fate of the sixteenth century Catholic Church. Once esteemed as the seat of both temporal and ecclesiastical authority and thought to be inviolate in body and law, its monolithic power began to crumble under the weight of one too many overt attacks. Martin Luther, frequently viewed as the man who single-handedly toppled the church from its pinnacle, was merely one more woodsman—if an important one—hacking away at an already besieged and corrupt infrastructure.

So it was with the throne of kingship. For centuries monarchical rule, a system that was thought to lend stability and continuity to pre-modern societies, had been the prevailing political order. And, although individual rulers might be assassinated, exposed to ridicule, or removed to places of imprisonment, the tradition of governance itself remained essentially unchallenged. Prior to the European revolutions of 1848 with their demands for new social and political agendas, the primary problems with this form of government involved the actions and personalities of the rulers. The basic question concerning the necessity for, or legitimacy of, autocracy were seldom openly debated.

Like all man-made creations, the role of the monarch was a frequently changing one, ever forced to redefine itself in order to accommodate to social, political, and religious realities. Even the Russian tsars, presiding over what appeared to be a compliant people, found it necessary to adopt the paternalistic mode and to behave with at least some measure of christian piety. Peter the Great's (1682–1725) refusal to do so embroiled him in what were undoubtedly his worst incidents of subject disaffection and sent a chilling message to other monarchs who may have wished to follow his despotic example.

By the mid-nineteenth century, most of the world's royalty governed not by fiat but through carefully constructed, power-limiting constitutions. Although they could still appoint—or dismiss—individuals in key governmental positions, or affect state policy through direct appeal to parliament or the people, the years of autocratic abuse were well on the way to extinction. Those few who behaved in such a way as to suggest that constitutional constraints did not apply to them inevitably ran afoul of the popular will sooner or later. Germany's Kaiser Wilhelm II (1888–1918) either evaded or haughtily ignored all limitations placed upon him with legendary intransigence. However, on those rare occasions when he was apprised that his words or his actions went against the grain of his people's beliefs and feelings, the kaiser was not above a bit of plebeian bowing and scraping. King Alexander of Serbia (1889–1903) should have followed Wilhelm's example. That he did not but that he continued with his constitutional excesses culminated in tragedy. Alexander and his equally unpopular wife were murdered by a contingent of their own troops, and their mutilated bodies were cast into the street before a cheering mob in the full light of day.

Some of the other rulers may have viewed their fall from a position of demigods as regrettable on the one hand but mildly relieving on the other. Abdul Hamid II (1876–1909) of Turkey, Mutsuhito of Japan (1867–1912), and Chulalongkorn of Siam (1868–1910) could begin to eliminate the ritual trappings that had kept their ancestors in silence and seclusion for centuries. While retaining some vestiges of semi-divine status, they (with the exception of the Chinese emperor) became sufficiently liberated to venture out into the world of mortal men.

The emergence of elected officials and government bureaucrats, the true designers of state policy, left the monarch free to pursue other interests, while still reveling in the mistaken assumption that control rested completely in the throne. Wiser rulers, like Austria's Franz Joseph (1848–1916), recognized early on that they were little more than glorified civil servants and foresightedly used their waning influence to intrigue for the fulfillment of their own agenda.

Clearly, monarchy was a complex system of governance peopled by equally complex individuals. Often led to decisions that reflected their diverse personalities and varying talents, the world's rulers were not a unified body of command. Instead, they represented, for better and for worse, a sort of random selection of humanity. Not always men or women of sterling character and sometimes lacking the intelligence necessary for their position, kings, queens, and emperors, nonetheless, were symbols of national identity. (National pride, obviously, might be a different matter.) As long as Germany had its kaiser and Russia its tsar, both countries experienced a continuing link with history. That the potentate had been greatly diminished in political stature, that he was frequently limited to the functions of admonishing, advising, and suggesting, was less important than the fact that his presence in the central position offered a sense of security.

"There Will Always Be an England" ran the popular refrain, followed in certain order by "God Save the King" or "Long Live the Queen." Then disaster struck. The shock, the dislocation, the death and disappointment occasioned by World War I acted as an ominous knell to the exalted ones. Their halo of majesty began to sink in an abyss of disillusionment. One by one, the great royal houses came tumbling down, shaken from their positions by political uncertainty and the unhealthy winds of war's reality. Hohenzollern, Romanov, and Habsburg were the first to crash, followed in succession by the aristocrats of the lesser German states. By the end of World War II more royal figures had joined the ranks of the unemployed, leaving less than two dozen reigning bluebloods.

In the decades since, the kings of Egypt and Greece and the Shah of Iran have been toppled. The remaining twenty-one include the following: King of Morocco, King of Lesotho, King of Swaziland, King of Jordan, King of Saudi Arabia, King of Nepal, King of Bhutan, King of Malaysia, King of Thailand, Queen of England, King of Spain, King of Belgium, Grand Duke of Luxembourg, Prince of Liechtenstein, King of Norway, Queen of Denmark, King of Sweden, Queen of Holland, Emperor of Japan, Prince of Monaco, and the King of Samoa.

Today's political pundits are in near unanimous agreement that the year 2,000 may not witness a single surviving monarch. Not one of the group (England it is conceded, and then only perhaps, excepted) is thought to be capable of lasting into the twenty-first century. At present, few of them perform more than ceremonial functions, and even fewer have any real power.

One optimistic thought may yet temper this portent of gloom. It appears that the fear and obedience that was once afforded to these figures has given way to something that may be less enduring but is no less real: fascination. Stripped of authority, shorn of power, many have managed to retain—or perhaps recapture—the mystique that set them apart. In their royal aura, they are viewed as objects of wonder and speculation, rather than anachronistic remainders of man's climb up the ladder of democratic self-actualization.

The postcards that illustrate this book tell us much about royalty, both politically and personally. For the part they do not reveal, we have history texts and biographies. And our own imaginations.

# About the Author

Jack H. Smith's keen interest in world history led him to select that field of study in college. But his preoccupation with the exploits of governments and the strengths and foibles of their rulers did not end when he received his bachelor's degree in Secondary Education. Now an avid collector of postcards, stamps, autographs, antique books, medals, coins, paper money, and historical documents, he has written many articles about these historical artifacts for well-known hobby and collector publications throughout the country.

*Royal Postcards,* published by Wallace-Homestead Book Company, is his first book. Jack, with his wife Sherry and their daughter Shanna, make their home in Cincinnati.

# 1

# Pricing and Rarity

One of the most difficult enterprises in writing a book on collectibles centers around the business of establishing a value guide. In the postcard field this problem is exacerbated by the fact that any given category may be rightly said to be more or less "popular" at a specific time. And as popularity, more than rarity, is—reputedly—the crucial factor to be considered when applying the price tag, the typical guide is at best a temporary expedient. For this reason the following scale seeks to depart from viewing these antiques in this manner. Instead, the aim has been to relate to royal postcards in terms of the relative difficulty a devotee may encounter in his search for them, and that both particularly and generally. The prices recorded here may be adjusted either higher or lower according to the fortunes of currency, while the rarity factors should remain constant.

It is with these cautions in mind that this rarity and pricing evaluation should be approached, and it is the author's hope that the reader exercise his own judgment in the perusal of these historical items, whose main function has always been to give pleasure and to inform rather than to enrich or deplete the wallet or purse.

R1   The lowest valuation for royal cards commonly encountered. Price range: $1–5.

R2   For cards frequently seen but always in demand. Price range: $5–10.

R3   Cards originally printed in large numbers but generally believed to be in limited supply. Price range: $10–15.

R4   Seldom-seen cards, many of which have a special historical or social significance. Price range: $15–20.

R5   Difficult-to-locate cards that are thought to have been printed in very small numbers. Also one-of-a-kind cards. Price range: $20–50+.

To each card herein pictured will be added, where pertinent, the following information: description or identification of picture including date if necessary, publisher or producer, coloration or type, and rarity factor.

# 2
# Early Cards

In 1899, a delightful tome entitled *Rulers of the World at Home* began its introduction this way:

> As being hedged about with pomp and circumstance, the conditions of royal life are ever a subject of peculiar interest. Reigning families constitute a class apart, and their manner of life presents accordingly a strong invitation to natural curiosity.

Indeed. What the author might not have known, writing as he did from a time when monarchy was everywhere in evidence, was why the last decade of the nineteenth century and the first two decades of the twentieth century occasioned such special interest in royalty. For, although the fascination level itself was greater or lesser at any previously selected time, during this particular period it reached unprecedented proportions. The reason for this is straightforward enough, although even the interested parties themselves may have had some difficulty identifying it.

The period from the late 1800s until 1918 represented what was essentially a twilight time of royal autonomy and perogative. Surprisingly, this was also a time of unsurpassed splendor and gaiety. Vienna's cafe society was in full healthy bloom, Germans idolized their pompous and outrageously flamboyant kaiser, and Englishmen of every stripe were alternatively humored and mildly alarmed by the life-style and antics of their animated monarch, Edward VII. The growth and prosperity of the middle classes, created by rapid industrialization fueled by ever-increasing overseas markets, created an atmosphere of leisure and well-being for those with the capital and social distinction to enjoy it. The upper echelons of landed gentry and the royalty touted and feted each other, while the lower social orders gazed on in wonderment or chagrin. Still, the very top of the progression ladder had room on its exclusive rung for one group only—aristocrats. And everyone knew it.

Elena, Queen of Italy. G. Modlano. Sepia. R4, $15.

During this era—a politically troubled one as shall be seen—the world's royal families were, in deed and in fact, a "class apart," and as such were accorded all the customary deferences. The imperial carriage was always given respectful right-of-way; curtsies, bows, and knee bending were done in the fashion prescribed; and royal appearances at functions were eagerly witnessed by teeming throngs jostling for position to catch a glimpse of his or her highness.

But, sociological analysis notwithstanding, the handwriting was already on the wall. Power-limiting constitutions and the creation of political parties with increasingly inflexible, radical ideals were formidable augurs positing a new social order. The monarchical system was in a state of decline, and everyone from the ruler down to the humblest peasant either knew it or felt it. Unable to slow the democratic surge pressing on all sides, royal personages accepted the last-minute adulation with the expected display of aloofness. Like dancers strolling to a familiar but tiresome waltz, the whole human cast—

ruler, politicos, merchants, peasants—kept step to what they recognized as the final musical chords.

There by the dozens to record these waning years for posterity (and profit) were the publishers of picture postcards. Photographers and artists of every shape, type, and inclination were salaried or commissioned to keep an inquisitive world apprised of everything connected with royalty. Public appetite for the cards was insatiable and universal. Citizens of democratically governed countries where titles of nobility were nonexistent also expressed a keen infatuation with these people about whom they knew so little. For many, postcards served as their first and only introduction to royalty, at least on a viewing level. Reading about them in the newspaper was one thing. Seeing real photographs and artist-drawn postcards of royalty was something else and much to be preferred. Posted from the countries of issuance, they were sent the world over and passed from hand to hand.

The question of who produced the first picture postcards has been the subject of heated debate, and the controversy has provoked several lengthy treatises. The ultimate answer may never be forthcoming, but the furor has been healthy for the deltiologist, and the research has helped increase his knowledge manyfold.

What has been identified are the first official "postal cards." The date of their production was October 1, 1869, and the issuer was the Austrian government. Sometime earlier, the North German Confederation had met in session to discuss the possibility of creating a government postal card and establishing a uniform price rate for it within the Austro-Hungarian Empire. The need for a smaller, less cumbersome piece of paper upon which a quick message could be written and which had the additional benefit of not requiring a separately affixed stamp had been acknowledged since the 1700s. And though the postal card would never completely replace the envelope-addressed letter, the quantity of sales, even from the very beginning, indicated the birth of a new passion. (It would later justifiably be referred to as a "craze.")

It was a small step from the government postal, with its unimaginative facade saved from total starkness only by the imprinted stamp, to the more heavily embellished picture card. However, this small step did not occur overnight. In fact, it was a full decade and a half more before these artistic and/or color-filled specimens would be seen in appreciable numbers.

Royal cards were among the last to appear, having been preceded by view cards, topicals, greetings, and the omnipresent advertising card. Sadder than the royalty card's late appearance was the fact that few of them were printed before 1900. Had it not been for the many marriages and special events that occurred during this period, even fewer would be available right now. Often acknowledged as the first royal postcards to be so identified are two mourning cards issued on the deaths of the two German emperors, Wilhelm I and Frederick III. (A card commemorating the 200th Bicentennial of the German Royal Family and picturing Wilhelm I with the dates 1861–1888, is believed to be of later manufacture and will so remain until an earlier postmarked one is discovered.)

It is not surprising that Germany would take the lead in producing royal postcards. The superior printing technology of Germany coupled with an internationally well known group of royal personages as subjects are the two primary reasons. Although Emperor Wilhelm II was also an important factor, we shall later discover most postcard books end the early or "pioneer" era in 1898. As that seems to be a reasonable cutoff point, this volume will continue the tradition. Regarding the valuation furnished for these cards, it should be borne in mind that the prices are general in nature. They do not reflect the increased worth that special factors of cancellation, special stamps, or significant messages may add to a specific card.

Because all of these early cards have undivided backs upon which only the address was permitted, many of the postally used specimens will have a mini-letter written on the picture side. To a few purists, these "ink spots," or even the cancellations themselves detract from the undisturbed innocence of the card. Most collectors seem to adopt a dissimilar stance; either they pay small attention to them or, as is most often the case, they accept the message as proof of the card's authenticity and hope that the writing or postmark relates to the person or event.

Here is a general list of many known cards and types dating from the early or pioneer era.

| | |
|---|---|
| 1888 | Mourning card for Emperor Wilhelm I. Black portrait at left, German postal. R5, **$50.** |
| | Mourning card for Emperor Friedrich III. Black portrait at left, German postal. R5, **$50.** |
| 1889 | Thirtieth birthday of Wilhelm II. Green and brown, German postal, portrait at left. R4, **$20.** |
| | Ascension of Wilhelm II. As above. R4, **$20.** |
| 1890–1898 | Ludwig II of Bavaria sleighriding. Lautz & Darmstadt. Black and white. R5, **$25.** |
| | Individual *Grüss aus* cards, usually related to military activities, with an inset of Wilhelm II or other rulers. R4, **$15–20.** |
| | As above, special occasion cards with insets of various rulers as part of montage. R4–R5, **$15–50.** |
| | Various individual rulers or royal personages. R4–R5, **$15–25.** |
| 1891 | Marriage of Prince Frederick August of Saxony to Louise of Toscana (Nov. 23). Separate insets of each at left, oversize government postal. R5, **$30.** |
| 1893 | Visit of the Russian fleet to France. Inset of tsar and ships. Black printing, postal. R5, **$50.** |
| | As above, large card, 4¾″×6″. In green, blank back. R5, **$50.** |

Wilhelmina, first Queen of the Netherlands. Coronation commemorative. Private issue. Sepia. R4, **$15.**

"Mad" Ludwig of Bavaria on a sleighride. Lautz & Isenbeck. Lightly colored. R5, **$20.**

**1895** Visit of Wilhelm II and empress to Jerusalem. Private card. R5, **$25.**

**1896** Marriage of Victor Emmanuel III of Italy to Princess Elena of Montenegro. Portraits at left in browntone. R5, **$25.**

As above, portraits in center. R5, **$25.**

As above, colosseum statue of Italia, red-brown. R5, **$25.**

As above, in blue. R5, **$30.**

Visit of Russian Tsar to France. Portraits and flags. Browntone. R4, **$20.**

As above, but in color with government stamp. R4, **$20.**

As above, large portraits. Purple. R5, **$40.**

As above, ships at Cherbourg. Colorful. R4, **$20.**

As above, portraits at left. R4, **$20.**

As above, tsarina and ships. R5, **$40.**

As above, portraits of tsar, tsarina, and president of France. R4, **$20.**

Seventieth birthday of Grand Duke Frederick of Baden. Colorful. Private card. R5, **$25.**

Berlin Exposition, portrait of Wilhelm II at left and views of exposition. Colorful. Private card. R4, **$20.**

Visits of tsar to various locations. On both private cards and postals. R4–R5, **$15–40.**

Prince Boris of Bulgaria. Portrait in center, red with five green stamp. Government postal. R4, **$20.**

As above with ten red stamp. R5, **$25.**

**1897** Centennial of Wilhelm I birth. Parade grounds and statue. Colorful. Goldiner, Berlin. R4, **$20.**

As above, different design. Stengel print, color. R4, **$15.**

As above, insets of Wilhelm I, Frederick III and Wilhelm II. Colorful. Goldiner, Berlin. R4, **$20.**

As above, insets and allegorical scenes. Black and white. Private card. R5, **$35.**

Visit of tsar to Coburg, portraits. R5, **$30.**

Victoria Jubilee, Egypt, statue, and lighthouse. Private card. R5, **$25.**

Victoria Diamond Jubilee. Portrait insets at left in red ribbon. Private card. R5, **$40.**

Brussels Exposition. Insets of king and crown prince. Colorful. Private card. R5, **$30.**

Return visit of French president to Russia. Multiple views in green, portraits at left. R4, **$20.**

Victoria Diamond Jubilee. Portraits of Prince Albert and Queen with Albert statue at right. Colorful. Private card. R5, **$50.**

Swedish Jubilee. King on green card. R5, **$60.**

Centennial of Wilhelm I birth. Revolving disc reveals emperor at various stages of his life. R5, **$60.**

As above, revolving disc showing Wilhelm II and family. R5, **$30.**

Sons of Wilhelm II in hiking clothes. Browntone. F. Kruis. R4, **$15.**

As above, different poses. Browntone with red printing. R4, **$15.**

Commemorative, Duke of Aumale. Castle and representation to left. Color. R4, **$20.**

**1898** Coronation of Queen Wilhelmina. Four portraits of statesmen on government postal, 2½ stamp. R4, **$20.**

As above, with five stamp. R4, **$20.**

Queen Wilhelmina in coronation robe, long view. Private card. Sepia. R4, **$15.**

As above, close-up. R4, **$15.**

Franz Joseph fiftieth year of reign, various types. R4–R5, **$15–40.**

Twenty-fifth year reign, King of Saxony, various types. R4–R5, **$20–40.**

Visit of Wilhelm II to Palestine and Turkey. Various types. R4–R5, **$15–25.**

One-hundred-fiftieth anniversary of von Thurn und Taxis. Insets of prince, princess and crown prince. Black and white with red and blue printing. R5, **$40.**

Duke of Aumale, commemorative, 1897. Private issue. Color. R4. $20.

King Wilhelm and Queen Charlotte of Württemberg. Embossed commemorative. Hockstetter. Color. R4, $15.

Wedding of Frederick of Weid to Pauline of Württenberg. Inset of couple at left in oval, building and scene to right. R5, $50.

Golden wedding anniversary of Grand Duke Frederick and Grand Duchess Luise of Baden. R5, $25.

Three German emperors. Embossed in ovals, colorful. Beger and Rockel. R4, $20.

Seventieth birthday and twenty-fifth year of reign, Albert of Saxony. Insets of king and queen to left, castle at right. August Franz. Colorful. R5, $25.

Elena, queen of Italy. Portrait at left. G. Modlano. Black and white. R4, $15.

1898    Souvenir of Belgian Congo Independence. King Leopold of Belgium at left with dignitaries in ovals underneath, railway to right. Ed Neli. Black and white. R5, $30.

Kaiser Wilhelm II and family members on horseback. Gustav Liersch. Black and white. R4, $15.

Kaiser Wilhelm II shaking hands with Bismark to left, bust of Wilhelm I in rear. Tulate. Sepia. R4, $15.

Coronation commemorative of Queen Wilhelmina of Holland. Picture in oval at left, crests at top, view of Gravenhage to right. Sepia. R4, $15.

King and Queen of Württemberg. Real photograph insets at left, crown above, crest beneath. Color. R4, $15.

In addition there are believed to exist many postcards related to the events detailed in the chapter on Special Occasions. Also not included in this list are most of the multiple cards of various monarchs and royal personages that were issued privately, by the government, and by the large firms. More cards are coming to light almost weekly, and this may continue to be the case for years.

**Production and Dating.** Unlike coins, stamps, banknotes, and other collectibles where production figures are given, the quantities of specific postcards printed are not always ascertainable. The problem is particularly acute in relation to the early material. Most of the pioneer producers, victims of the general malaise in the industry that occurred after World War I, are no longer conducting business. Records are, therefore, next to impossible to locate. Add to this the fact that many cards were reprinted or pirated by other firms at later dates, and the task of computing printing quantities becomes difficult and complex.

Which brings us to another problem, that of determining actual dates of manufacture. If many publishers were hesitant about identifying themselves on their cards, they were even more reluctant to specify dates. In those instances where an event is historically recognizable, the issue would appear to be easily resolved. Unfortunately, it must be acknowledged that not a few cards were printed after the pictured event. Before 1903, most European cards had undivided backs, which does help pinpoint early cards.

Nevertheless, some measure of caution should be exercised when inspecting this early material. It is known that counterfeits of some of the more expensive cards have made their way into the marketplace. For this reason, many collectors prefer to purchase postally used material as a means of insuring authenticity. At present, the problem of spurious issues is not one of serious proportions. Ongoing investigations and the preponderance of assiduously detailed checklists have aided in unraveling the dating controversy, rendering it also less troublesome. However, there is one precaution collectors should take at all times: Use only the services of a reputable dealer.

Anyone who has ever made a conscious effort to collect royal postcards will readily agree that the early ones are extremely difficult to locate. Not only were they

Centenary of Wilhelm I's birth, 1897. Private issue. Sepia, R5, **$35.**

Prince Boris of Bulgaria, 1896. Government issue. Color. R4, **$20.**

Two of Wilhelm II's six sons. A. Ackermann. Sepia. R4, **$15.**

Dowager Empress Victoria of Germany, the oldest child of England's Queen Victoria, she was mother of Wilhelm II. L. Klement. Sepia. R4, **$25.**

Italy's Queen Mother, Margherita. Eliotipia Molfese. Sepia. R4, **$15.**

Wilhelm II in idealized, stilted pose. A. Hildebrandt. Browntone. R4, **$15.**

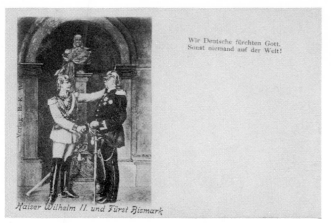

Wir Deutsche fürchten Gott.
Sonst niemand auf der Welt!

Kaiser Wilhelm II. und Fürst Bismark

Wilhelm II with Bismarck, the "Iron Chancellor." An obvious propaganda card, as Wilhelm had replaced Bismarck a few years earlier. B.K.W.I. Sepia. R4, **$15.**

produced in very limited numbers, but attrition has also exacted a toll, leaving few survivors. Being constantly in demand, they spend little time gathering dust in dealers' stocks. But it is not scarcity and age alone, important though they be, that make early royal postcards such desirable items. Many collectors and connoisseurs find their appeal is closely linked to the fact that they can be viewed through the microscope of historical credibility, and having been so examined and measured, are not found to be wanting. Unlike some period memorabilia where the connection to history is less immediate, royal postcards represent a direct connection between subject and object. They offer the viewer a look, sometimes an intimate one, at the people themselves. With their aid the years vanish, and we are swiftly ushered into those august presences that are no more.

# 3
# Royalty Around the World

Prince Imperial, born 16th March, 1856, killed in Zululand 1st June, 1879, transferred to Imperial Crypt, Benedictine Abbey, Farnborough, 9th January, 1888.

Prince Imperial Eugene Louis Jean Joseph Napoleon of France. Killed in romantic fashion in the Zulu War, 1879. Reproduction. R2, $10.

For many people, the image of royalty is a multifaceted one. Glittering jewels and fabulous wealth are an indispensable part of that vision; so too is the mental picture of individuals whose very isolation forces a kind of self motivation and attendant aloofness.

Like many images, the portrait is flawed, being at once both more and less than the reality. To be sure, royal figures were and are a distinct breed. Separated from the common folk by circumstances of birth, by life-style, and by destiny, they had to be different. Their environment was dissimilar to that of everyone else just as surely as the set of expectations involving them were different. They were regarded as exotic islands in a sea of banality, a perception obviously more valid in the past than in the present.

The first royal personages paved the path down which they have all trod. In this sense, the remaining royalty are victims, trapped by protocol and held prisoner by the perceptual matrix that has been created about them. Of course, it's not a bad life and the cell is hardly a dingy one. . . .

It is this blend of fantasy and fact that maintains the luster and perpetuates the mystique surrounding their majesties. The postcard images in this book are not intended to dispel the mystery (as if such a thing were possible). Instead, it is hoped that they may stimulate the viewer to proceed along avenues of personal research and enlightenment. More will be said—and shown—of individual rulers and royal characters in later chapters. For now, it may suffice to sample the variety.

**The Monarch as a Military Figure.** From the days of antiquity, countries have been ruled by sovereigns who regarded themselves as their countries' supreme military commanders. Even Japan with its shogun and China with its tradition of imperial seclusion were not excepted, because final disposition in all temporal affairs fell within the purview of the exalted ones. It was a title and a designation that few monarchs were willing to abrogate under any circumstances. Their visages, adorned in military splendor, replete with a panoply of accoutrements graphically illustrating the glory of victory and the prestige of battle were the subjects of countless works of art. One particularly engaging slate artifact discovered in the

African desert depicts the famed pharoah Narmer, reputedly the first ruler of a unified Egypt, grasping the hair of a kneeling captive and preparing to inflict a mortal blow with a mace clutched in his upraised fist. Obviously considered worthy of emulation, the pose was recreated 1500 years later by another pharoah with equally warlike tendencies, Thotmes III.

Macedonia's hero, the battle hungry and acquisitive Alexander the Great, is best known to succeeding generations for his feats of conquest. So immense was Alexander's military reputation that his dream of uniting the ancient world under his rule with the intellectual blessings of Greek civilization seems overshadowed. The remnants of a mosaic from Pompeii, a copy of a Hellenistic work executed in 300 B.C., pictures a youthful Alexander arrayed in full battle gear, an unsheathed sword at his side, leading his troops to battle astride the legendary steed, Bucephalus. Not to be outdone, profiting perhaps from this example, Rome's Caesars saw to it that both their coinage and their statues displayed the proper military connection.

Era followed era and one leader gave way to another without fundamental alteration in the schematic. Only the names changed. For the most part, the mind-set remained the same. How much responsibility for this should be attached to the rulers themselves or what amount should be ascribed to a nation's people who demanded strength and forcefulness as well as justice and moral rectitude from its leaders is a question that may never be answered. But it is worth noting that the appellation "The Great," when applied to the name of any monarch (Alexander, Frederick, Peter, and Catherine come readily to mind), had an almost cause-effect relationship to war and conquest.

**The Hohenzollerns.** Unquestionably the chief proponent (as well as trendsetter for other royal personages) of the military look among twentieth century monarchs was Germany's aggressive, bombastic leader, Kaiser Wilhelm II. Although the fact does not speak to Wilhelm's defense, it may be surmised that he came by his propensity in honest fashion. Relative newcomers to the kingly estate, the Prussian Hohenzollerns were, by and large, a feisty group, ever ready to fight or to intrigue for inquisition and attention.

Frederick II ("The Great," 1740–1786) was the first, if not the only Prussian king whose personal achievements are historically significant. Like most accomplished rulers, he was a man of many parts. An admirer of the philosopher Voltaire, who was his frequent dinner guest, Frederick insisted on retaining his own counsel and acting from his own passions. Considering his accomplishments, the decision could hardly be called an altogether poor one. Frederick reorganized and expanded the Prussian treasury, initiated much needed legal reforms, launched new industries, built roads and canals, and introduced improved methods of farming. He welcomed disparate groups of people the world over to his kingdom. By the end of his reign Prussia's population had increased by more than 250,000 and included French Huguenots expelled by Louis XIV, Jews, Jesuits, and even Turks for whom he promised to build mosques. In all, Frederick was well deserving of the adjective "enlightened." The term "despotic" was also most appropriate. By doubling the size of his army (into which he poured four-fifths of the national income) to a strength of 150,000 and making it an instrument of his sometimes cruel will, he was able to defeat the armies of France, Austria, and Russia. In all areas of state policy, Frederick had the authority to give or to take away, and he did not permit friend or enemy to forget it. In a moment of pique he uttered a most personally revealing statement: "I will sustain my power or let everything perish so that even the name of Prussia will be buried with me."

By comparison, his successors were men of little importance and lesser merit. With but one exception, they had identical militaristic tendencies, but all lacked Frederick's insights and political ingenuity. Even the first German emperor, Wilhelm I (1861–1888), the famed victor of the Sadowa and Sedan campaigns, was scarcely more than an elevated Prussian Junker. The wisest decision he ever made—and it took considerable prompting— was to place his fortunes in the capable hands of the German Empire's true architect, Prince Otto von Bismark. It was due chiefly to the "Iron Chancellor's" efforts and adroit manipulation of foreign policy that Wilhelm became the first emperor (also and mainly called "kaiser") of a unified Germany.

Unfortunately, the man who could have had the greatest impact on the German ship of state as it blustered and pushed its way into the twentieth century was allowed to languish unnoticed for too long and to die too soon. Frederick III (1888) was everything his ancestoral namesake was not. Kindly disposed, though sufficiently Prussian to be gruff of voice, he was Germany's one hope for liberal reform. Had "Fritz" as he was affectionately called, not died from cancer of the throat a mere ninety days into his reign, World War I might never have become a reality. Moreover, Germany's relations with France, Russia, and England would assuredly have been less strained. Unpretentiously modest, good-natured, but not especially gifted intellectually, Frederick married the Princess Victoria, eldest daughter of England's Queen Victoria. Trained by her studious, methodical father, Prince Consort Albert, "Vicky" was a child prodigy able to converse fluently in several languages at an early age. She was well-schooled in politics, art, music, science, and religion and she became an excellent mentor to her husband. Under

Alphonso XIII and "Ena," the King and Queen of Spain. Rotary. R3, **$15.**

Portraits of Franz Joseph at various stages of his imperial life Red Cross card. Color. R3, **$15.**

her tuteledge, which included lectures and repeated remonstrances on the evils of autocracy, Fritz came to believe that his rule needed to represent a turning away from the old order. There can be little doubt that he would have led the German people into a period of political and industrial progress. Without his leadership, Germany was to experience the latter on an unprecedented scale but was to find itself sadly lacking in the former.

The blame for this may be squarely laid at the door of his son and heir. If Frederick represented the positive, Kaiser Wilhelm II clearly stood for the negative, and in no one single aspect of his personality was this more evident than in his choice of dress. Such was Wilhelm's attachment to military attire that he personally designed dozens of uniforms and insignia for his army and navy, always careful to retain the most ostentatious outfits for himself. It was said that he could strut even when standing still. But the chin forcibly and rigorously upthrust, the perpetually tightened spine, and the glowing glint in Wilhelm's steel gray eyes betrayed a basic insecurity and an attendant need to posture.

"The kaiser wants to be the bride at every wedding and the corpse at every funeral," professed a popular statement, spoken only half in jest. Whatever the occasion, Wilhelm could be counted on to have a uniform for it. Indeed, he seldom failed to dress in what was recognized as a predictably inappropriate style. Among his more than three hundred costumes was one of a German high admiral that the kaiser insisted on wearing to a stage production of *The Flying Dutchman*. (He was barely— and just barely—dissuaded from dressing as a Roman general for the formal opening of a museum of antiquities.) The immense cupboards that housed his evergrowing wardrobe were tended by an official keeper who had under him a number of assistants, including two tailors that occupied themselves almost exclusively with the care of the buttons.

From Wilhelm's perspective, the invention of the camera could not have occurred at a more opportune time. For, although it predated him and captured the faces of earlier folk, none seemed to bask in it with quite the same relish. Wilhelm met each refinement of the camera with delight. Because it fed his need for social approbation, Germany's warlord seldom missed an opportunity to foist his presence in front of the magical black box.

That Wilhelm was lacking in emotional maturity and manifested a sense of inferiority is too well documented to need further proof here. What is still debatable is the issue surrounding the kaiser's feelings about his "deformity." A dwarfed left arm, the result of being wrenched from his mother's womb during a difficult childbirth, left the young prince in a poor position to accomplish some of the physical feats of normally limbed children. His mother admitted finding the arm a loathesome sight, an observation the manifestation of which would not have gone undetected by Wilhelm himself. And though he adapted himself remarkably well to his condition and became a better than average marksman and rider, he still had to have his dinner meat cut for him all through his life. A propensity for hunting expeditions that frequently included a kind of ritualized slaughter of the captured game, was only one mark of the kaiser's compulsion to display his manhood. Perhaps more revealing was his relationship with the camera. He wanted his picture taken as often as possible but remained ever conscious of his image. He preferred to pose with the offensive left hand hidden in the security of his coat pocket or clutching the hilt of his sword, elbow slightly bent, thus making it appear closer to normal length. Artistic renditions invariably depicted both of the kaiser's arms of equal size. In those instances when another presence is in the painting, Wilhelm's arms frequently appear to be longer than the other person's. Whether this was on Wilhelm's orders (doubtful) or the result of the artist's discretion (probable) is an issue of conjecture.

Victoria Louise and German Crown Princess Cecilie. N.P.G. R3, $15.

Swedish king with Finland's president. R3, $15.

Nothing pleased the All Highest (Wilhelm's favorite, self-chosen title, omission of which could lead to unpleasant consequences) quite so much as the act of presenting a picture or postcard likeness of himself to friends and subordinates. That the recipients were in no position to refuse the gift, in fact that they could do little except thank him profusely with bows, intonations of "Your Majesty," and looks of adoration, never occurred to the kaiser. Sometimes these presentations became spectacles themselves, "grist for the mill," with another camera in attendance to record and immortalize the event.

Properly polished and festooned with ribbon and rope, Wilhelm goose-stepped across the European stage in grandiose style. As he barked orders in his assertive, dictatorial manner, he may not have known that half the world considered him a clowning buffoon, while the other half viewed him as a reckless neurotic and decidedly dangerous. Of some significance is the fact that he fared much better in the eyes of his people. While his advisors debated about whether to placate or manipulate him, the bulk of the German population reacted to him with a combination of reverence, good humor, obedience, and exultation.

His potential six million man army (a number representing not only those on active service, but reservists and others considered to be of recruitment age), easily the largest of the continent, served to increase his neighbor's apprehensions. For Wilhelm, the army represented an irresistible opportunity to expand his self deceit. Almost singularly lacking in intellectual endowment, unable to entertain even the rudiments of diplomatic behavior (except when it suited his purposes), and infused with a vision of himself as "Emperor by Absolute, Divine Right," he played the part of Caesar to the hilt, seemingly oblivious to any would-be Brutuses that might be waiting in the wings.

It is of significance that many of the kaiser's biographers have been pleased to perpetuate one of his particular con-

ceits. In book after book, Wilhelm II has been portrayed as intelligent, if not intellectual. In truth, and according to the results of any common sense analysis, the reverse is what is revealed. Although it is indisputable that the kaiser was cunning and that his memory for detail was just short of amazing, it is generally agreed that these attributes are hardly the substance and full parcel of which intelligence is composed. Indeed, no man who is incapable of seeing beyond his own passions or who is unable to comprehend the merits of divergent viewpoints or who cannot recognize the difference between personal prejudice and objective reality can be called intelligent. Wilhelm saw no distinction between Divine will and his own.

In short, Wilhelm II might have been complex in his personality and his motivations, but his intelligence appears to be, at the very most, mediocre.

Sadly, Wilhelm's limited mental gifts did not keep other nobility from copying his life-style and his manner of dress. Many of the lesser German aristocracy were quick to follow his lead, draping themselves with military garments of every description. This was all the more true of the younger nobility. The older crowned heads scarcely needed the prompting, having worn their own uniforms in actual battle. Saxony's King Albert, like many of his fellow monarchs, had already distinguished himself militarily before the kaiser's birth. However, off the parade ground and the battlefield, his deportment was akin to that of Bavaria's ruler, Ludwig III. Both wore the commander's cloth but maintained a mild-mannered, peaceful bearing. This was not the case with their progeny and heirs. Most of them adapted to the custom too well, the kaiser's son-in-law Ernst August being an arrogantly perfect example.

To the enthusiast of royal postcards, all present interesting characters worthy of investigation. But it is to Wilhelm II that the collector returns, and for good reason. Not only is his postcard portrait the closest to comple-

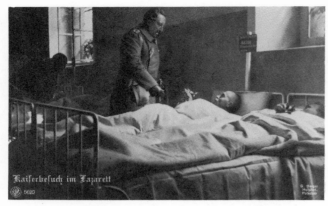
Wilhelm II visiting the sick during World War I. Seemingly an unfeeling man the Kaiser kept his personal anguishes to himself. N.P.G. Sepia. R3, $15.

tion, attested by the multiple thousands of them that have been devoted to him, but he is clearly the most intriguing of the lot. While most of the material depicts the kaiser in an autocratically rigid stance, in some ways almost a caricature of himself, there exists those few cards where a different aspect of the man, even of the military man, can be examined.

It is here where one sees him as doting commander concerned with the welfare of his troops and the foodstuffs they are eating. Here that he is pictured with bended knee and head bowed in prayer. Here that one encounters an angry kaiser arguing with his generals against the unrestricted use of submarine warfare. Nor should these uncharacteristic glimpses be casually dismissed as propaganda tools, although that was obviously their intended purpose. Wilhelm could be—and was—headstrong, impetuous, verbose, and ruinously indelicate in speech and action. "I wish we could put a padlock on his mouth," was one of his mother's statements. But he could be, not unlike some of his fellow monarchs who had similar swings in mood and temperament, congenial, compassionate, and willing to please or amuse. A man of extremes, Wilhelm's chief personal flaw was an all-encompassing ability to delude himself. He envisioned his role as that of supreme leader, in a sort of partnership with God, although it was not always certain that the Diety had the commanding position. God was referred to by Wilhelm as "The Highest," while Wilhelm, as mentioned earlier, claimed the distinction of "All Highest." One anecdote tells of the kaiser emerging from the chapel where it was reported that The All-Highest had conferred with The Highest. Obviously the story either confuses the issue of the chain of command or it clarifies it, depending upon one's perspective.

Wilhelm's models were Frederick the Great, his grandfather Wilhelm I, and Bismarck, a man too much like himself to be retained in a position of authority. In all too few situations did the humanity of his father or the intellectual prowess of his mother manifest themselves, and on those infrequent occasions when they did, the results were negative. They went against the mind-set of the man who grasped the imperial reins with this saber-

rattling proclamation: "We are bound together—I and the army—so we are born for one another and so shall we hold together indissolubly, whether as God wills we are to have peace or storm."

**The Habsburgs.** Although it is a fact that almost half of the royal postcards printed prior to 1920 were those of various German aristocracy (with perhaps 25 percent of the remainder being British), those of Austrian nobility represent no small number. Germany, with its head start in the publishing of multicolored cards and an emperor who was seldom averse to the presence of the camera or easel, had ample cause for being in the lead.

Autstria was a different matter. The primary reason there are so many postcards of Austrian royalty had little to do with the size and geographical importance of the Austro-Hungarian Empire, although this revelation may seem strange to students of history. Instead, the answer is to be found in the person of the Empire's ruler, the bewhiskered and docile-appearing Franz Joseph. A monarch for sixty-eight years (1848–1916), his reign was of longer duration than any of his contemporaries, exceeding even that of Queen Victoria by almost half a decade. The rest of the world, especially the non-European part, wanted a look at this venerated old rascal who assumed his imperial status during the 1848 revolutions and retained it through every upheaval and disastrous military campaign that plagued his tenure. A less well liked ruler or one less committed to his duty as a servant of the people might not have endured for so long. But the emperor was well regarded and respected by both friends and adversaries.

As for his own inclinations, it would be difficult to ascertain whether Franz Joseph considered himself a military man with political responsibilities or a political leader with military obligations. One thing is certain: He did not require assistance or example from Germany's Wilhelm II in the selection of his attire.

For decades Franz Joseph had restricted himself as much as possible to two forms of dress. One was his everyday military uniform, worn occasionally with a plumed hat, an accessory donned more for tradition than for adornment. The other was a simple Tyrolean outfit consisting of hiking shoes, lederhosen supported by galluses, knee socks, shirt, and an unbecoming hat. He wore this outfit when hiking or hunting, his two favorite forms of relaxation in later life. On rare occasions demanding more elaborate apparel, which might include white gloves and a ribbon sash across a coat emblazoned with medals and special headgear, the emperor seemed to be in a hurry to conclude the festivities and proceed to whatever state business awaited him.

He had not always been this way. As a young man Franz Joseph sported a pompadour hairstyle, well polished and distinguished looking boots, and close fitting coat and trousers. He loved to attend the opera and to give grand ballroom parties where he would waltz away the evening hours with his young and beautiful bride,

Empress Elisabeth. Unfortunately, this interlude was brief. The carefree atmosphere quickly vanished under the pressures of mountains of paperwork, imperial borders that were ever being readjusted after his numerous wars, and the demands of multiple subject nationalities that never ceased chattering about political autonomy. In addition, the army, if not an actual passion of his, did at least demand sizable chunks of his time and energy. The empress, who was not emotionally stable even under the best of circumstances, could ill-tolerate what she came to view as abandonment by her increasingly duty-bound husband. Her pleas that he spend more time with her were ineffectual, although her tantrums upset Franz more than she could have known. Eventually, fueled by nervous urgency and a desire to be free to pursue her myriad interests, she departed for foreign ports. At first her jaunts were brief and the reunions joyous, but Elisabeth would soon grow impatient to be off once more in pursuit of warmer climates and freer air. Finally the emperor himself began to realize that neither love nor family responsibility was sufficiently compelling to keep his wife by his side.

Elisabeth ("Sissy") took her husband's gaiety with her, but to his credit and everyone's amazement, Franz Joseph managed to retain his remarkable vigor to the end of his long life. Confining himself henceforth (with the excepting distraction of Katarina Schratt about whom more will be said later) to the business of state, Emperor Franz dressed for the job. Even family gatherings, unless they dealt with religious or civil events, failed to bring about any alteration in his attire. Special ceremonies called for a bit of grooming improvement but, as time wore on, they became less in number, and shorter in duration, and more to his liking.

The sixty-five archdukes and archduchesses who were related to the emperor are harder individuals to classify. A few were dilettantes of a sort, but most were not. Rudolph, the emperor's son, had been something of a dandy during his early years, but his suicide prevents posterity from learning what kind of ruler he might have been. The ill-fated Franz Ferdinand, next in line to the throne, was also atypical. Dour of demeanor, Franz cared less about his appearance than about his politics. As it happened, they were generously tinged with a federalistic liberalism, which curiously did not stay the assassin's bullet from penetrating his flesh or that of his wife, the morganatic Countess Sophie Chotek. The last ruler of Austria-Hungary, Emperor Carl, was even more liberal, but he was also a royalty conscious Habsburg and not averse to dressing in royal style or, if he thought the circumstances required it, acting with regal pomp. In Carl's case, however, the strain of autocracy was weakened water. His main concern was not for personal glory but rather for the benefit of the various subject races within the empire. All told, the Habsburgs were a disparate lot. The one constant among them, the ladies of course excepted, was a fondness for military costumes. Few successfully evaded the affectation.

The Emperor Franz Joseph is somewhat easier to characterize. He was a taciturn, spartan individual given more to silent resignation and determined political maneuvering than to emotional outbursts. His postcard portrait is pretty much in keeping with his personality. The earth tone grays, blues, and browns of his military cloth tell of a man with little time for merriment and none for foolishness. Once, when Kaiser Wilhelm II was in attendance at an Austrian military exercise, he sent his aide to request some champagne. "Let him drink beer," mumbled the emperor. The story, whether true or not, was revelatory of the man.

With his adored grandchildren Franz Joseph was soft-spoken, the kindest of patriarchs. Nor did he fail to be deferential to women. He likewise had a measure of compassion for the poorest of his subjects, as indicated by several legendary tales of his largesse. But when it came to work or business, he was of one piece and that was a different cloth. In dealing with his generals, his ministers, even his fellow monarchs, the emperor was often cruelly abrupt. The very manner of his death is symbolic of his life-style. He died at his desk, demanding, between fits of coughing occasioned by an attack of bronchitis, that some state papers requiring his signature be brought to him immediately.

**The Saxe-Coburg Windsors.** In the year 1900, there was no shortage of occupied thrones among the world's great powers. Today, only one remains: Great Britain's. Although reduced in status to a nebulous commonwealth of nations rather than a substantive empire upon which the sun never set, Great Britain still retains a position of respect. Of the few remaining monarchies, it may truthfully be stated that none of them, even in their heydays, enjoyed a standing in the international community as elevated as Great Britain's.

Undoubtedly, a large part of the reason for this is related to England's cultural contributions. Shakespeare, Bacon, and Samuel Johnson are not easy men to forget. Nor, in the political sphere may one ignore Henry VIII, James I, or Elizabeth I. But all these names and by inference, deeds, signify something greater, something called monarchical tradition. Great Britain is admired because, save for one small span of eleven years, she has kept her sovereign through good times and ill for almost twelve hundred years. And she may keep her royal family for another twelve hundred years for an even simpler reason—their popularity.

For approximately one hundred and fifty years, or roughly since the ascension of Queen Victoria, the love of the British people for their monarch has been truly remarkable. While most palaces are devoid of occupants, the English are pleased to pay whatever is necessary to maintain their queen—or king—in a handsome state of royal splendor. Victoria, Edward VII, George V, George VI and Elizabeth II have all basked in the light of public favor, and future rulers may reasonably expect the same benevolence. Even the short-reigned Edward VIII managed to sustain the warm feelings of a people he shocked and disappointed by his abdication and marriage to the commoner, Wallace Simpson.

Again, the rationale that explains this is easy to follow. More than any other nineteenth or twentieth century monarchs, the British sovereigns graciously deferred to public opinion and bent to the popular will. Queen Victoria (1837–1901) set the tone by relinquishing one royal perogative after another until she had reduced her political status to that of chief advisor. This position was one in which she felt most comfortable, in that it allowed the queen to express her thoughts in a forthright style that became her trademark. And Britain listened to their diminutive first lady, a fact not lost on her various prime ministers. Intently poring over state papers, often late into the night hours, and questioning everything that came within her sight, Queen Victoria earned the reverent regard of her subjects. Her personal conduct was considered to be a model of propriety. While her grandson, Kaiser Wilhelm II, raved, ranted, and grandstanded, she applied herself to her duties in an exemplary fashion.

The same may be said of her style of dress. Victoria may have been a monarch but she was also a lady who attired herself in unassuming style. This lack of ostentation applied to the crown as well. She wore it only when absolutely necessary and then with self-conscious stiffness. The postcards bearing Victoria's likeness display the image of a ruler who didn't need to wear military clothing to earn respect. Her attitude and approach to life were enough to guarantee that end. The royal die of politically acceptable behavior, in England if not elsewhere, was cast by her, and her descendants reaped the imperial benefits. Even Victoria's effervescent eldest son Edward VII (1901–1911) was more like her than might be suspected. Although of different personality, he wisely followed his mother's political lead, permitting the real business of the state to be conducted by Britain's elected officials.

The nervously energetic "Bertie" has often been categorized as a good-natured rogue. His much publicized extramarital dalliances, deplorable as they now seem, were but one facet of a man whose passions were exceeded only by his girth. A prodigious epicure and nonstop cigar smoker, Edward was seldom less than fondly thought of by the typical Britisher. The aristocracy enjoyed being at parties and afternoon teas when their jovial king was in attendance, and the working classes delighted in their good-hearted monarch's public appearances. They roared with and at Bertie's antics, sure he was one of their own, at least in temperament and inclinations.

However, another side of Edward VII's character, which biographers fail to recognize, did exist. Behind the sincere smile and the warmth of his effusive laughter resided a man who accepted the gravity of his position. Those few who stepped beyond the limits of propriety and became overly familiar with his majesty were quickly brought to toe. He was Bertie, sometimes; at all times

he was the King of Great Britain, a fact best not to be forgotten by his court favorites or anyone else. In this regard, Edward was every inch his mother's son. And he regarded the crown with its attendant titles just as seriously as did any of his contemporaries.

Nor was Edward remiss in dressing the part. His favorite portraits were those that depicted him in military attire, not because he was aggressive or war-oriented, but because they projected an image of strength. If there was an area in which he displayed vanity, it was here. Artists who painted the king in military regalia were certain to make him appear a bit leaner, trimmer, and broader of shoulder than was actually the case. There is, of course, the other side of the coin. It might be an oversimplification to suggest that Edward deliberately chose to exhibit a martial exterior in order to balance his basically gentle nature. But there is some measure of truth to the statement. Sharing the royal stage with him were as bellicose a group of fellow monarchs as anyone might ever have the misfortune of meeting, so Bertie found it expedient to do a little posturing. The king had no intention of ruling over an empire that would be regarded as second class in any way.

Edward did not live long enough to test Britain's stamina for war. But his progeny, George V (1911–1935) and George VI (1935–1952), were rulers during times of international conflict. It is interesting, at least in the case of the first George, that military vestments became the cloth for all seasons, worn in good times and ill. George V seemed to relish wearing them, although he could slip with ease, like other cultured English gentlemen, into hunting garb at the first suggestion of a sporting event. George VI was less inclined to wear uniforms during his reign. This seems slightly odd, considering his abbreviated career during World War I as an airman who exhibited a fair share of derring-do and adventurous exuberance. In any event, his contact with World War II does not appear to be as intimate as was his father's with the earlier cataclysm.

If the postcards of them are any indication, it is reasonable to assume that many of Britain's royal figures during this century and the last were as comfortable out of military threads as they were in them. This hypothesis is borne out by the countless photographs of the aristocracy in traditional tweeds or silken cloth. It may be that they felt quite secure on a throne that had been well warmed by centuries of continuous use. Few of their royal cousins could luxuriate in such prestigious lineage.

**The Romanovs.** Anyone who knew Nicholas II (1896–1917), the last Russian tsar, when he was a child might easily have predicted what sort of ruler he would become. Gentle of voice and manner, easily manipulated by his mother (later by his mistress, and then his wife), and terrified of his authoritarian father, little Nicky was clearly lacking in the necessary requisites of the true autocrat.

It wasn't because he didn't put forth the effort. In fact, Nicholas wanted nothing more out of life than to be an acceptable tsar and to please those he loved. Even if it were possible to accomplish both aims simultaneously, Nicholas was not the man to see success in the endeavor. He didn't have it in him as a child, as a military cadet, or later, as a ruler when the destiny of the Russian state rested on his shoulders. His was the soul of a poet. And though he could display callousness when the blood of his starving people was the issue, such infrequent behavior was his only manifestation of the inherent strength of his ancestors. In other respects Nicholas was simply unable to follow the pattern they had set.

Borne from the fires of adversity, tempered by war and internal conflict, and hardened in the snows of Siberian winters, Russia's tsars were a genuinely impressive lot. Most had hair-trigger tempers, and all were political gamblers of one sort or another. Ivan the Terrible (1547–1584) and Peter the Great (1682–1725) are but two examples from a long list. The oft-repeated quote from John Milton's *Paradise Lost* about preferring to "rule in Hell" rather than "serve in Heaven" might fairly describe the philosophy of a greater part of them. Theirs was a military mentality, strengthened by the divine right of kings' theory and religious beliefs that seem strange to modern practitioners of Christianity. And, whether tracking game for sport or cavorting on the battlefield, they fixed their souls and eyesight on a single vision—conquest.

How and why Nicholas II deviated from this persona is, to some extent, unknown. That he did is fact. Adding irony to this turn of events was the open acknowledgment that the tsarist Russia of Nicholas's time was the most autocratic of all European monarchies. The heir-apparent's training should have been sufficient to make him a strong ruler when he ascended the throne. It included the obligatory military training to which Nicky applied himself, but the results did not produce a man with a noticeable flair for leadership or genius for tactics. He did develop a knack for making friends. Unfortunately, most were little more than drinking companions and of small value to him in later life.

In uniform the tsar cut what must have been considered a dashing figure, trim of beard and slender of build. However, a closer examination reveals a man better suited to captaining a cruise vessel than to leading an army into combat. In fact, the tsar felt much more at ease commanding the royal yacht than when reviewing his troops. He did spend considerable time with them, even taking command of the army during World War I, but he never became a soldier. The postcard pictures of him are weighted in favor of Nicholas the family man, a role and a perception that undoubtedly pleased him. Nicholas, the long-suffering husband and indulgent father, would have made an excellent member of the rural middle class, leading a pleasant yet nondescript life.

Russia's last tsar never learned that wearing military clothing and being a military person were not the same thing. His kindly, doe-like eyes betrayed a softness and indecisiveness that led him and the Russian state to a disaster beyond undoing. Had he understood that it was possible to find a median ground between the harshness of his predecessors and his own temporizing talent, the history of twentieth century Western Civilization might have been writ in different letters.

**Other Monarchs.** One of the lamentable facts that must be attached to Wilhelm II's propensity for military attire is that so many of the world's royalty sought to emulate him. Whether they—or he—maintained the discipline that is presumed to go with the cloth was not deemed important. And thereby lies a tale or two for historians. Were this fashion copying contained solely within Germany, it might have represented a less troublesome state of affairs. But it was not, and the ripple effect seemed to touch, if not contaminate, virtually every corner of the globe. Turkish sultans, Scandinavian kings, even a few Indian maharajahs were only too ready to array themselves in specially designed military outfits. That such a peace loving, normally level-headed soul as Siam's Chulalongkorn could wear a uniform as easily and comfortably as his ancestors had worn the more traditional robes of satin breeches (or is it silk pajamas?) is disquieting. Gone were the multicolored vestments and glittering, gaudy accoutrements by which the Eastern monarchs of earlier ages had been identified. In their place ribbons, ropes, and assorted honorary buttons glared from haughtily expanded chests covered by the rigid tailoring of a wool or cotton uniform coat. That the bulk of India's princes did not adopt this wardrobe standard merely pointed to the sad truth that their attitude was perceived, even in bygone days, as anachronistic.

The postcard arrived too late to monitor the transition, catching it instead in full stride. By the last half of the nineteenth century, royal military attire was no longer just another change of clothing donned when attending field exercises or addressing the troops. It had become the dress to wear on any occasion, in all situations and habitations in western Europe. Before the turn of the century, due in no small part to the influence of Wilhelm II, many of the world's royal families had begun to follow suit. Although few went to Wilhelmian extremes, most thought that the uniform added something to their stature. Moreover, they comported themselves with increased dignity and gravity when thus outfitted.

One may reasonably wonder if these uniforms were helpful in creating an aggressive orientation. One has less cause to question whether the fashion lent legitimacy to military ideals.

From about 1800 to the end of World War I, it is obvious that monarchy frequently paraded itself across the world stage with military bearing and precision. The postcards tell us that the music to which they stepped was that of the belligerent drum.

King Nicholas of Montenegro. World War I had ended his reign and autonomous existence of country. Rotary. R3, **$15.**

Ludwig of Bavaria in full military splendor. Martin Herpich. Reproduction. Color. R3, **$10.**

King Carlos I of Portugal who was assassinated with the crown prince in 1908. Rotary. R3, **$10.**

Empress of Japan. Rotary. R4, **$15.**

Emperor Yoshihito of Japan. Underwood and Underwood. Color. R3, **$10.**

Nicholas II, Russia's last tsar. An unlikely military man. Rotary. R3, **$15.**

Russian Empress Alexandra Feodorovna (Alix) in happier days. Rotary. R4, **$20.**

Queen of Portugal and wife of Carlos I. S.I.P. R3, **$15.**

Franz Joseph, an unfortunate but dedicated patriarch. B.K.W.I. R2, **$10.**

The Sultan of Zanzibar. Note medals, a concession to European tastes. A.R.P. de Lord. Browntone. R4, **$20.**

Victorio Emmanuel II, first king of a united Italy. N.R.M. Reproduction. Black and white. R2, **$10.**

Alexander I, Serbia's boy-king who was assassinated in 1903. S.I.P. Browntone. R4, **$20.**

Albert I of Belgium. Black and white. R3, **$15.**

Victor Emmanuel III, Italy's diminutive king. VAT. Black and white. R2, **$10.**

Edward VII of England. Valentines. Color. R2, **$10.**

Rajah of Pudukota. Beagles. R3, **$10.**

Draga Masin, Serbia's unpopular queen, who was assassinated with her husband. S.I.P. Browntone. R4, **$20.**

Abbas Pasha, Khedive of Egypt. Royal title but no royal power. Black and white. R3, **$15.**

Austria's ill-fated Empress Elisabeth. B.K.W.I. Reproduction. R2, **$10.**

Manuel II, King of Portugal. Rotary. R2, **$10.**

Crown-Princess Louise of Saxony. B.K.W.I. R3, **$15.**

Augusta Victoria ("Dona"), the German Empress. Her devotion to Wilhelm II "passed all understanding." Gustav Liersch. R2, **$10.**

Queen Elisabeth of Belgium. An unpretentious sovereign and a dedicated nurse during World War I. V.G. R2, **$10.**

Princess Mary of Hannover. A.u.H. Brunotte. R3, **$15.**

Queen Alexandra of England. "National" series. Color. R2, **$10.**

Crown-Prince Rupprecht of Bavaria. Muller. R3, **$10.**

Prince Heinrich (Henry) of Bavaria. R3, **$15.**

The Emperor of China. O. Ludwig. Black and white. R4, **$20.**

Queen Wilhelmina in national costume. Speelman. R2, **$10.**

Ernst August, King of Hannover. Brown-tone. R4, **$15.**

H. H. THE MAHARAJA BAHADUR, KASHMIR.

Maharaja of Kashmir. Dutta. Sepia and white. R3, $10.

Prince Harold of Denmark. Eneret. R2, $10.

H. M. QUEEN OF HOLLAND & PRINCE CONSORT

Queen Wilhelmina and prince consort in riding habit. R2, $10.

King of Württemberg. Hockstetter & Vischer. R4, $15.

Queen of Württemberg. Hockstetter & Vischer. R4, $15.

Kaiserin u. Königin v. Österreich u. Ungarn

Empress Zita of Austria-Hungary. Sepia. R3, $15.

Prince Ernst August of Brunswick in uniform of Death's Head Hussars. Gustav Liersch. R3, **$15.**

Marie Adelaide, former Grande Duchesse of Luxembourg. She died as a nun while still in her twenties. Rotary. R3, **$15.**

Prince George of Sweden in naval uniform, an ever-popular outfit of all Swedish nobility. Stender. R3, **$10.**

King Peter of Serbia, successor of the assassinated Alexander I. His acceptance of the crown caused quite a stir. Beagles. R3, **$10.**

Wife of Prince August Wilhelm of Prussia. Headgear is typical of type popular with female royalty of the time. Photochemie. R3, **$10.**

Princess Clementine of Belgium. Her marriage to Prince Victor Napoleon of the House of Bonaparte was opposed by her family. V.G. R3, **$15.**

King Prajadhipok of Siam (Thailand) reigned from 1925–35. He was educated in England and France. R4, **$15.**

Princess Maria, second daughter of Ludwig III of Bavaria, with daughter. Percy Hein. R4, **$15.**

Queen Victoria of England taking her oath to maintain the protestant faith. Reproduction. R2, **$10.**

Grand Duke Adolphe, founder of the Luxembourg dynasty. R5, **$35.**

William III, King of Holland until 1890. Reproduction. R2, **$10.**

Prince August Wilhelm, one of Wilhelm II's six sons. Wilhelm Kohler. R3, **$10.**

Sweden's Princess Maria. Axel Eliasson.
R3, **$10.**

Queen Marie of Hannover. A.u.H.
Brunotte. Browntone. R3, **$15.**

Prince August Wilhelm, son of Wilhelm
II, and friend. Photochemie. R3, **$10.**

King Constantine and Queen Sophie of
Greece. Sophie was the sister of Emperor
Wilhelm II. Black and white. R2, **$10.**

Princess Sophie of Oldenburg, wife of
Eitel Friedrich, another son of Wilhelm
II. Rotophot. R3, **$15.**

Queen Mother of Italy in mourning for
her assassinated husband, King Humbert
I. R3, **$15.**

Crown Prince Rupprecht of Bavaria. Artist-drawn. R3, **$15.**

A realistic portrait of Wilhelm II. R3, **$10.**

Idealized painting. WRB & Co. R3, **$15.**

A remarkably accurate representation of the kaiser. Note the glaring eyes. R3, **$15.**

A propaganda painting of the kaiser as a determined looking military commander. R3, **$10.**

A seldom-seen portrait. Hermann Wolff. R4, **$20.**

Another painting superbly executed. B.K.W.I. R4, **$20.**

Kaiser Wilhelm II. Tuck Oilette. R3, **$10.**

Propaganda card involving the kaiser. M. Munk. R3, **$15.**

Franz Joseph, well-acquainted with trouble and sorrow. WRB & Co. R3, **$15.**

Memorial card of Franz Joseph, 1916. R3, **$15.**

Popular portrait of the venerable old Habsburg. Von Christoph Sohne. R3, **$10.**

Abdul Hamid of Turkey. Rulers of the World. R2, **$5.**

Ferdinand of Bulgaria. Rulers of the World. R2, **$5.**

Wilhelmina of the Netherlands. Rulers of the World. R2, **$5.**

Mohammed Ali Shaw of Persia. Rulers of the World. R2, **$5.**

Prince Albert of Monaco. Rulers of the World. R2, **$5.**

Prince Chun, Regent of China. Rulers of the World. R2, **$5.**

Mutsuhito of Japan, Rulers of the World. R2, **$5.**

Peter I of Serbia. F.H. Altman Rulers of the World, 1909. R2, **$5.**

Edward VII as Colonel-in-Chief of the Household Cavalry. "Trim and Fit." Gale and Polden. R3, **$15.**

Edward VII on a state visit to France. In embossed insets are king and French President Loubet, 1903. R3, **$15.**

Coronation series for Edward VII, 1901. Tuck. R3, **$15.**

Another coronation card of George V, 1911. Tuck. R2, **$10.**

Lilioukalani with her daughter. South Seas Curio Company. R4, **$15.**

Coronation series for George V, 1911. Tuck Oilette. R2, **$10.**

Lilioukalani, last Queen of Hawaii. South Seas Curio Company. R4, **$15.**

Prince Regent Luitpold with signature. R3, **$15.**

King William II of Württemberg. Hermann Schott. R4, **$20.**

King William II of Württemberg. Embossed. Von Hochstetter. R4, **$20.**

Victor Emmanuel III. Valentines. R2, **$10.**

Victor Emmanuel with advisors. World War I related. Embossed. R3, **$15.**

Victor Emmanuel. Exquisite and delicate color by Guggenheim & Co. R3, **$15.**

Queen Elena of Italy. Another Guggenheim offering. R3, **$15.**

Hawaiian Coat of Arms. Island Curio Store. R4, **$15.**

Twenty-fifth anniversary, reign Prince Regent Luitpold of Bavaria, 1911. Government issue. R4, **$15.**

Prince Luitpold, ninetieth birthday commemorative, 1911. R4, **$20.**

Italian royal family. R2, **$10.**

Emperor Maximillian of Mexico. His reign was brief. Reproduction. R2, **$10.**

Queen Elisabeth of Belgium in a painting honoring her war contribution. R3, **$15.**

Twenty-fifth wedding anniversary King of Württemberg, 1911. R4, **$20.**

Napoleon in imperial splendor, 1804. A.N. R2, **$10.**

Emperor Yoshihito of Japan with special cancellation. R5, **$50.**

Empress of Japan with imperial children. Special cancellation. R5, **$50.**

Hirohito, last Emperor of Japan. R4, **$20.**

Marriage of Queen Wilhelmina of the Netherlands to Prince Henry of Mecklenburg, 1901. R4, **$20.**

Wilhelmina in royal attire. Valentines. R2, **$10.**

One hundredth anniversary, birth of Wilhelm I, 1897. J. Goldiner. R4, **$20.**

A member of India's nobility. Looking at a world fast disappearing. R2, **$10.**

German and Austrian Crown princes, "Little Willy" and Carl. FH & SW. 1915. R2, **$15.**

Marriage of Queen Wilhelmina of Holland. R4, **$20.**

36

Wilhelmina in more conventional clothing. Dr. Trenkler Co. R2, **$10.**

The Countesses of Savoy, 998–1416. R4, **$20.**

Duke Ferdinand of Austria, World War I-related. R3, **$15.**

Duke Ferdinand as an army commander. R3, **$15.**

The Child Emperor of China. R5, **$50.**

Karl IV, the title for several kings and emperors of various countries. Note that the scene might be a representation for any of them. R1, **$5.**

Emperor Carl (Karl) of Austria-Hungary. Coronation commemorative, 1916. S.V.D. R3, **$10.**

Emperor Carl as a military man, a position he was ill-prepared to fill. Von Christoph Sohne. Facsimile signature. R3, **$15.**

"The King's Drama." Supposedly insane Ludwig II of Bavaria was Richard Wagner's patron. R5, **$25.**

Chinese Emperor with advisors. In reality the political power in China resided with the dowager Empress Tz'u Hsi. R5, **$50.**

The crowned heads of Europe. Underwood and Underwood. R2, **$10.**

Twenty-fifth anniversary, death of Ludwig II, 1911. R3, **$15.**

One hundredth anniversary, birth of Wilhelm I, 1897. J. Goldiner. R4, **$20.**

Mohammed V proclaimed Sultan of Turkey, 1909. R4, **$20.**

German Empress. One of the beautiful Stengel cards. R3, **$15.**

German Emperor. Stengel. R3, **$15.**

Queen Elena of Italy. Stengel. R3, **$15.**

Napoleon I. Another magnificent Stengel. R2, **$10.**

Alphonso XIII. A colorful offering from Valentines. R3, **$15.**

Queen Victoria Eugenia of Spain in a dress befitting royalty. R3, **$15.**

Oscar II, king of Sweden until 1907. R3, **$10.**

Three generations of Swedish royalty: Oscar II, Gustav V, and Gustav VI. Axel Eliassons. R2, **$10.**

Prince Oscar (later reigned as Gustav VI) and his fiancée, Princess Margaret of Connaught. Rotary. Color tinted. R2, **$10.**

One hundredth year of royal reign in Baden. Also fiftieth anniversary of King Friedrich and Queen Luise, 1906. Government issue. R4, **$20.**

Twenty-fifth year of reign, Albert of Saxony, 1898. Gebr. Knauss. R5, **$20.**

Twenty-fifth year of reign, Albert of Saxony, 1898. Aug. Brunning. R5, **$20.**

King Haakon VII of Norway; Queen Maud, and Crown Prince Olav. R1, **$5.**

Queen Louise of Denmark, 1907. R3, **$15.**

King Ferdinand of Bulgaria, a military die-hard. R4, **$20.**

Ferdinand of Bulgaria. His dream, to capture Constantinople. S.V.D. R4, **$20.**

Princess Helen of Greece. R4, **$20.**

In this painting Wilhelm II's left arm is made to appear longer than Franz Joseph's. Frederick O. Walter. R3, **$15.**

German Crown Prince Wilhelm with facsimile signature. R3, **$15.**

Wedding of German Crown Prince, 1905. R4, **$20.**

Franz Salvator, husband of Austria's Marie Valerie. Red Cross card. R3, **$15.**

Twenty-fifth year of reign and seventieth birthday, 1898. R5, **$20.**

King Constantine of Greece and family. R3, **$15.**

King Constantine on a patriotic card. R4, **$20.**

Brussels Exposition of 1897 with insets of King Leopold II and Crown Prince Albert. R5, **$30.**

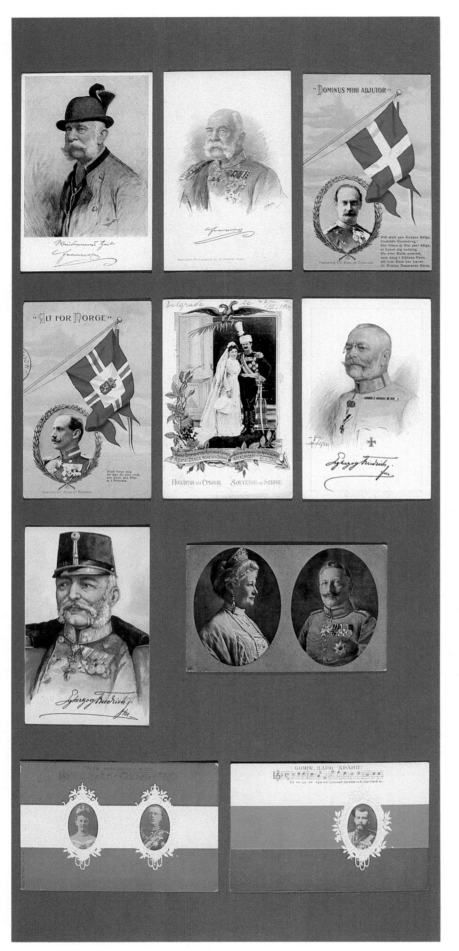

A docile appearing Franz Joseph in Tirolean garb. M. Munk. R3, **$15.**

Another artist-drawn, royalty signed card. Red Cross. R3, **$15.**

Flag card with Denmark's Frederik VIII inset below. R2, **$10.**

Flag card portraying Haakon VII of Norway. R3, **$10.**

The ill-starred marriage of Alexander of Serbia, 1900. R5, **$30.**

Prince Friedrich in uniform. Von Christoph Sohne. R3, **$15.**

Prince Friedrich of Austria. R3, **$10.**

Wilhelm II and Empress Augusta Victoria. R3, **$10.**

Ruler insets, Queen and Prince Consort of Holland, R3, **$15.**

National song card. Tsar Nicholas II in embossed inset. R3, **$15.**

Crown Prince Constantine of Greece. Rotary. R2, **$10.**

British Princess Royale, Mary. Rotary. Tinted. R2, **$10.**

Nicholas II of Russia. Medals but no exploits. Rotary. R3, **$15.**

Queen of Rumania. Writing under the pen name "Carmen Silva," Queen Elisabeth was an accomplished poetess, writer, and musician. C. Sfetea. R4, **$15.**

Prince Alexander, Duke of Saxe-Coburg Gotha. During World War I, the duke's family was forced to relinquish their "too German" sounding name. J.J. Samuels. R2, **$10.**

Sultan of Morocco, Mohammed-Ben-Youssef. A dying breed of royalty. R4, **$20.**

Napoleon III, last Emperor of France, sepia reproduction of a painting. R2, **$10.**

Christian X, King of Denmark. An unpretentious sort of ruler. R2, **$10.**

The King and Crown Prince of Korea. Tinted. R5, **$35.**

Prince Ernst August of Brunswick. He married Victoria Louise, only daughter of Wilhelm II and was given the territory of Brunswick-Luneburg as a wedding present. Photochemie. R2, **$10.**

Prince Regent Luitpold of Bavaria. Luitpold assumed the Regency after King Otto was declared mentally incompetent. Jos. Paul Bohm. R2, **$10.**

King Peter of Serbia wearing a combination of royal and military attire. This was in pattern with past Serbian rulers. Underwood and Underwood. Color. R3, **$10.**

King Constantine of Greece. Geschwister Moos. R2, **$10.**

King Manuel of Portugal. Beagles. R2, **$10.**

King of Spain as an admiral. Tuck Oilette. Color, artist-drawn. R3, **$10.**

Greek Crown Prince George. R2, **$10.**

Prussia's Prince Oscar. R2, **$10.**

Austrian Duke Friedrich. R2, **$10.**

King Friedrich August of Saxony. Friedrich Grober. Artist-drawn. Color. R3, **$15.**

King George V of England. A popular, common-sense monarch. Beagles. R1, **$5.**

Prince Friedrich of Austria in field marshall's uniform. B.K.W.I. Artist-drawn. Color. R3, **$15.**

King George V on horseback. Samuels, Ltd. R2, **$10.**

Emperor Carl of Austria-Hungary. Artist-drawn. Color. R3, **$15.**

Prince George of Greece. Black and white. R3, **$15.**

Austrian Duke Franz Salvatore. He married Marie Valerie, daughter of Emperor Franz Joseph. B.K.W.I. R2, **$10.**

Victoria Louise, only daughter of Wilhelm II, in uniform of Death's Head Hussars. Photochemie. R3, **$15.**

German Crown Prince in close-up view of Death's Head Hussars' headgear. Photochemie. Black and white. R3, **$15.**

Italy's Duke of Abruzzi, a military hero. Guigoni & Bossi. R2, **$10.**

Crown Prince Gustav of Sweden. Aktiebolags. Color. R2, **$10.**

Enigmatic King Edward VII of England. Tuck's. Artist-drawn. Color. R2, **$10.**

German Crown Prince. Gustav Liersch. R2, **$10.**

Wilhelm II with "Bird of Paradise" helmet. Photochemie. Black and white. R3, **$15.**

Wilhelm II in a typically haughty stance. Rotophot. R3, **$15.**

Wilhelm II in one of his many military uniforms. Note the withered left arm. Photochemie. R3, **$15.**

Crown Prince Rupprecht of Bavaria, a royal figure with an interesting life. Artist-drawn. Color. R3, **$15.**

Franz Joseph in prayer, presumably requesting military victory. Rotophot. Artist-drawn. Sepia. R3, **$10.**

Prince Oscar, one of Wilhelm II's six sons. R3, **$15.**

Prince Adelbert of Prussia in a naval uniform. Photochemie. R2, **$10.**

King Ludwig III, last ruler of Bavaria. Percy Hein. R3, **$15.**

Crown Prince Rupprecht of Bavaria conferring with one of his subordinates during World War I. Wilhelm Wassmann. R3, **$15.**

Chulalong Korn, King of Siam (Thailand). He was the son of the king immortalized in the Broadway musical. Rotary. R3, **$15.**

King Albert of Belgium with French General Foch. P. Houstraas. Sepia. R3, **$15.**

The Duke of Connaught. G. D. & D.L. R2, **$10.**

King Albert I of Belgium, the soldier-king of his small country. Rotary. R2, **$10.**

King George of Saxony ruled for only two years before his death. R3, **$15.**

Crown Prince of Morocco as colonel of the guard. R3, **$15.**

The later-assassinated King Carlos of Portugal. Beagles. R3, **$15.**

Franz Joseph. Artist-drawn. Color. R3, **$15.**

Prince Consort of Holland. E. Bieber. R2, $10.

King Haakon VII of Norway. Rapid Photo. R1, $5.

King Victor Emmanuel III of Italy. Beagles. R2, $10.

Prince Heinrich of Reuss, a minor German royal house. R4, $20.

Prince Max of Baden. Bruder Kohn. R3, $15.

King of Denmark, Frederick VIII. Rotary. R1, $5.

Franz Joseph and Franz Ferdinand. Sepia.
R3, **$15.**

# 4
# Royal Families

One of the least explored historical areas of royalty has been the relationship between the monarchs and their families. This is regrettable, for not only would such observations portray the rulers as more than one-dimensional characters but such examination would, in many cases, help to illuminate their public personas. Wives, children, mothers, fathers, sisters, brothers, aunts, uncles, and cousins were more than simply blood relatives of royal figures; they were royalty themselves. Of equal significance, their association and encounters with the monarch impacted on the molding of his personality.

Wilhelm II may be offered as primary support for this thesis. Although the kaiser was generally the same sort of dictatorially abrupt person with his children as he was with his subordinates, he behaved differently with his mother and his wife. A quiet, almost unnoticeable woman, Wilhelm II's wife was easily intimidated by her forceful, overbearing husband. However, it was this very acquiescence and adoration that created his problems. To escape her companionship during the evening hours, the emperor sought refuge and solitude in state papers and international newspapers. Wilhelm preferred this political dabbling and rumination to the boredom of engaging in what he considered senseless chatter with the empress. When questioned by her, the kaiser would quickly respond, "You don't understand these things" and return to his reading. Thus, his proclivity to magnify both his and Germany's importance in the international community was enhanced—and that with disastrous results—because his wife was not the kind of companion who could divert him from his own worst tendencies and faults.

That Wilhelm II could be manipulated by a shrewd, discerning woman, one with the wisdom to know which strings to pull (and when to pull them) is evidenced by the kaiser's relationship with Hermine, his wife in exile. Both Wilhelm's mother and his first wife could have profited from her example. So obviously could several world leaders.

The German imperial house. Photochemie. R2, $10.

Conversely, his mother, Kaiserin Victoria, established the tenor of their relationship in his youth, and it was one of criticism and disapproval. Unable to appease or satisfy her, Wilhelm came to despise her liberal thinking and to detest the enlightened social philosophy of the England that she represented. From such attitudes and misunderstandings are history created.

Another ruler (of decidedly more modest pretensions than Germany's warlord) whose family relations were significant was Italy's diminutive king, Victor Emmanuel III. Princess Elena of Montenegro, his youthful and energetic bride, was the perfect helpmate, and Victor seldom failed to treat her or their children with respect and kindness. Sometimes stern and demanding with his progeny in the matter of their education, he took considerable pains to shower both them and Elena with praise and encouragement. As the exploits of his courage on the battlefield during World War I and the firmness he displayed in removing Benito Mussolini from power during World War II demonstrated, Victor Emmanuel could be as serious and determined as circumstances dictated. But when the time was ripe for family picnics, scenic drives through the countryside or excursions to foreign countries, the

Birth of German crown prince's son. Gustav Liersch. R2, **$10.**

Prince Oscar of Prussia with family. Gustav Liersch. R3, **$15.**

Prince Ferdinand of Bavaria with family. The prince was a physician. R4, **$20.**

Wife of Bavarian crown prince with daughter. J. Windhager. R3, **$15.**

king was willingly prepared, camera at the ready (Victor Emmanuel was an excellent amateur photographer) to involve himself with family and friends in a thoroughly enjoyable fashion.

To find the royal parent who outshone all royal parents in his doting concern for wife and family one would have to turn to the least likely of countries and look at the most unexpected residence. For it is in Russia, that geographical configuration of Europe and Asia, and in its tsar, Nicholas II, that one will find exemplified the very essence of filial softheartedness. (Some would say softheadedness as well.) The contrast of harsh Russian winters and damp, forbidding castles as a backdrop against which the effusive warmth of Nicholas's relations with his wife and children was displayed is an inviting one to explore. Totally devoted to his empress wife and able to find his full range of emotions only through her and their progeny, the last tsar of all the Russias became a marionette to be played and plucked, by her and others, into the most unseemly and ridiculous of positions.

Nicholas had the spirit of a pliable peasant when a will of iron would have been more suitable, and compensated for this misfortune by using harsh, autocratic measures when restraint and understanding were what was required. His indecisiveness, combined with a desire to placate his wife and her circle of friends (including that unrepentant holy man, Rasputin) led him time and again into situations that eventually proved his undoing. But through it all one can observe the almost total lack of deceitfulness, the boyish charm, the true innocence, leaping out from postcard photographs of Nicholas II with his beloved family.

Occasionally, although not often enough, the photographer might catch a monarch unaware and thus be in an enviable position to capture a truly intimate glimpse of the royal personage. Photographs of this nature are relatively rare and reveal something about the private person that the ceremonial pictures fail to show. But even the formally posed pictures with family and friends are not without considerable value. In the hands of historians, all of these portraits become implements that facilitate character reconstruction.

To collectors of royal postcards, they also serve as reminders that royalty was sometimes humane and all too human. From the monarch as ruler, to the ruler as national symbol, to the national symbol as household member, the line of pictures needs only the image of him as recreational creature to flesh-out the complete person.

Four generations of the Bavarian royal house. Percy Hein. Sepia. R3, **$15.**

Duke and Duchess of Saxe-Coburg Gotha and family. J.J. Samuels. R2, **$10.**

Franz Ferdinand with his family. Bruder Kohn. R3, **$15.**

Daughters of Luxembourg's William IV. Two of them were to become grande duchesses of the small country. R4, **$20.**

Prince Ernst, son of Franz Ferdinand, Austrian heir apparent. B.K.W.I. R4, **$20.**

Dowager Queen Margherita of Italy with her mother. Guigoni & Bossi. R3, **$15.**

The King and Queen of Portugal. Rotary. R3, **$15.**

Crown Prince Rupprecht of Bavaria and family. Percy Hein. Sepia. R2, **$10.**

Archduke Franz Ferdinand with his beloved family. R4, **$20.**

Crown Prince Constantine of Greece with his children. Beagles. R3, **$10.**

The Duke and Duchess of Connaught with their extended families. Rotary. R3, **$15.**

Princess Marie Valerie, only daughter of Franz Joseph, with husband and children. E. Lerch. R2, **$10.**

Alphonso XIII of Spain with his son. A proud father, the king was not a model husband. Rotary. R2, **$10.**

King Christian X and Queen Alexandrine of Denmark. Rotary. R1, **$5.**

Dutch royal family and queen mother. J.H. Schaefers. Black and white. R2, **$10.**

Princess Juliana of the Netherlands with her grandmother. R3, **$15.**

The Belgian royal family. Tuck. R2, **$10.**

Princess Marie Jose, daughter of Albert of Belgium and later wife of the last king of Italy. R2, **$10.**

The Youngest Hohenzollern. Son of the German crown prince. J. Wollstein. R3, **$15.**

Crown Princess of Sweden and children. Beagles. R2, **$10.**

King and Queen of Norway and Crown Prince Olaf. Philco. R2, **$10.**

Children of Italy's Victor Emmanuel III. Sepia. R2, **$10.**

King Ernst August of Saxony and son. Klinkhardt and Eyssen, R3, **$15.**

The Duchess of Connaught with daughters. Rotary. R3, **$15.**

Princess of Wales and her two sons. Left, the future Edward VIII. Beagles. R2, **$10.**

Emperor Franz Joseph with his grandchildren. B.K.W.I. R3, **$15.**

Early picture of Wilhelm II with family. Black and white. R3, **$15.**

A rare early photograph of the Russian royal family. R4, **$20.**

Princess Juliana of Holland. Beagles. R3, **$15.**

Son of the German crown prince in military regalia. Gustav Liersch. R3, **$15.**

# 5

# Special-Occasion Cards

Among the most avidly sought—and jealously guarded once they are obtained—of all royal cards are those that fall into the "special occasion" category. Weddings, births, deaths, coronations, and commemoratives of every description come under this broad heading, and they are frequently snatched from dealers' stocks with what amounts to gleeful abandon. The wealth of them is such that the collector may literally spend years accumulating specimens without greatly disturbing the supply. In instances where entire sets and series, especially of the more significant events, have been printed, few royalty collectors are immune to "completion" mania as they strive to locate the one card that may finish a series. Then they realize that that set is only one of many and the quest starts anew. Of even more interest are those individual cards that may represent the only photographic or artis-

tic reminder of a special event. These particular rarities increase the joy of the hunt and expand the pride of ownership.

Thankfully, memorabilia of this type was rapidly generated by an almost never-ending chain of events. And what a selection there was from which to choose. Photographers and artists were ever busy clicking and painting away, trying to satisfy the demands of those anxious for postcard souvenirs. As with many other categories of postcards, Germany, England, and Austria produced the lion's share of special occasion material. And yet other countries were not remiss in this area and are not to be overlooked. The following list of events for many of which postcards were produced, provide an overview of the variety and may serve to whet the appetites of even those with only a passing interest.

Coronation of George V, 1911. L.L. Black and white. R1, $5.

Coronation of George V, 1911. L.L. Black and white. R1, $5.

# Coronations and Ascensions

Coronation of George V, 1911. L.L. Black and white. R1, $5.

Carl's coronation as last King of Hungary, 1916, in Budapest. B.K.W.I. R5, $35.

**1888** Frederick III, German emperor, March 9

Wilhelm II, German emperor, June 15

**1889** Alexander of Serbia, king, July 2

Carlos of Portugal, king, October 19

Menelik II of Abyssinia, emperor, April

**1890** Adolphe of Luxembourg, grand duke, regency established April 11 (installation as sovereign July 23, 1891)

Wilhelmina of Holland, queen. Regency established November 23–24 (installed as sovereign November 23, 1898)

**1891** Liliuokalani of Hawaii, queen, January 20

Wilhelm II of Württemberg, king, October 6

**1892** Abbas Pasha of Egypt, khedive, January 7

**1894** Abdul Aziz of Morocco, sultan, June 7

Nicholas II of Russia, tsar, (crowned May 26, 1896)

**1900** Son of Prince Tuan of China, installed as imperial successor, January

Victor Emmanuel III of Italy, king, August 11

**1901** Edward VII of England, king, August 8

**1902** George of Saxony, king

**1903** Peter I of Serbia, king, June 15 (coronation September, 1904)

**1904** Frederick August of Saxony, king

**1905** Frederick VIII of Denmark, king, elected King of Norway, November 13

William IV of Luxembourg, grand duke, November 22

**1906** Haakon VII of Norway, king, June 22

**1907** Mohammed Alim of Persia, shah, January 19

Gustav V of Sweden, king, December 8

**1908** Mulai Hafid of Morocco, sultan, January 11

Manuel II of Portugal, king, February 2, 1908

Ferdinand of Bulgaria, tsar (he had formally been king), October 5

Infant heir-apparent proclaimed Chinese Emperor, regency established under Prince Chun, December 21

**1909** Mohammed V of Turkey, Sultan, April 27

Ahmed Mirza of Persia, shah, July 16

Albert I of Belgium, king, December 23

**1910** George V of England, king, May 7 (coronation at Westminster Abbey June 22, 1911)

Prince Nicholas of Montenegro, king, August 28 (after Montenegro declared a kingdom)

**1912** Christian X of Denmark, king, May 12

Marie Adelaide of Luxembourg, grande duchesse, June 18

Yoshihito of Japan, emperor, July 30

**1913** Constantine of Greece, king, March 19

Installation of Ernst August and Victoria Luise (Emperor Wilhelm II's daughter) as Duke and Duchesse of Brunswick, May 14. (At this time, which was their wedding day, the kaiser re-established the monarchy at Brunswick as a wedding present)

Ludwig III of Bavaria, king, November 12

**1914** Wilhelm of Weid accepts throne of Albania, February 21

Ferdinand of Rumania, king, October 14

**1916** Carl of Austria-Hungary, emperor, December 12

**1917** Alexander I of Greece, king, June 12

**1918** Boris III of Bulgaria, tsar, October 5

Mohammed VI of Turkey, sultan, July 6

Peter I of Serbia becomes King of Yugoslavia, November 24

**1919** Charlotte of Luxembourg, grande-duchesse, January 15

**1920** King Constantine of Greece returned to throne by plebiscite, December 19

Feisal (also spelled Faisal) of Syria, king

**1921** Emir Feisal (same as Feisal of Syria) crowned king of the new kingdom of Irak (Iraq or Mesopotamia), August 23

Alexander I of Yugoslavia, king, November 5

1922    George II of Greece, king, September 28

Ferdinand of Rumania, king, October 15 (return to throne)

1923    Ahmad Faud of Egypt, king, when British Protectorate withdrawn

# Abdications and Expulsions

**1889**    King Milan of Serbia, March 6 (abdicated)

Emperor Pedro II of Brazil, November 15 (dethroned)

**1893**    Queen Liliuokalini of Hawaii, January 7 (dethroned)

**1900**    Emperor of Korea forced into abdication by Japanese, July 19 (abdication)

**1909**    Sultan Abdul Hamid of Turkey, April 27 (deposed)

Shah Mohammed Alim of Persia, July 16 (dethroned)

**1910**    King Manuel II of Portugal, November 8 (dethroned)

**1911**    Prince Chun, Regent for Chinese Emperor forced to abdicate, December 1 (abdicated)

**1912**    Child Emperor of China, February 12 (abdicated)

**1913**    "Mad" King Otto of Bavaria, November 5 (deposed)

**1914**    Wilhelm of Wied flees Albania after rebels bombard the capital, May 28

**1917**    Tsar Nicholas II of Russia, March 15 (abdicated)

King Constantine of Greece, June 12 (abdicated)

**1918**    Ferdinand of Bulgaria, October 5 (abdicated)

King Boris of Bulgaria, November 2 (abdicated)

King Frederick August of Saxony, November 8 (abdicated)

King Ludwig III of Bavaria, November 8 (abdicated)

Emperor Wilhelm II of Germany, November 9 (abdicated)

After World War I virtually all the German states adopted republican forms of government following massive abdications and expulsions of their rulers

King Nicholas II of Montenegro, December 2 (forced abdication)

**1919**    Grande Duchesse Marie Adelaide of Luxembourg, January 9 (forced abdication)

**1920**    King Feisal of Irak (forced to abdicate)

**1922**    King Constantine of Greece abdicates a second time, September 27

Sultan Mohammed VI of Turkey, March 16 (deposed)

**1924**    King George of Greece, March 24 (deposed)

**1925**    Crown Prince Carol of Rumania renounces throne and is succeeded by his four-year-old son, Prince Michael, December 31

# Deaths

**1888**    Wilhelm I, German emperor, March 9

Frederick III, German Emperor, June 15

**1889**    Rudolph, Austrian Crown Prince, January 30 (suicide?)

John of Abyssinia, king, April 3 (slain by Dervishes)

Luis I of Portugal, king, October 19

**1890**    Amadeus I, ex-king of Spain, January 18

William III of Netherlands, king, November 23

**1891**    Kalakaua of Hawaii, king, January 20

Charles I of Württemberg, king, October 6

Pedro II, ex-emperor of Brazil, December 5

**1892**    Tewfik Pasha of Egypt, khedive, January 7

**1894**    Muley Hassan of Morocco, sultan, June 7

Alexander III of Russia, tsar, November 1

**1896**    Nasir-ed-din of Persia, shah, May 1 (assassinated)

**1898**    Elisabeth of Austria, empress, September 10 (assassinated)

**1900**    Umberto I of Italy, king, July 29 (assassinated)

**1901**    Milan, ex-king of Serbia, January 29

Victoria of England, queen, January 22

**1902**    Albert of Saxony, king, June 19

**1903**    Alexander of Serbia, king, June 10 (assassinated)

**1904**    Isabella of Spain, ex-queen, April 9

George of Saxony, king

Murad V of Turkey, ex-sultan, August 29

**1905**    Sergius of Russia, grand duke, February 17 (assassinated)

Adolphe of Luxembourg, grand duke, November 14

**1906**    Christian X of Denmark, king, January 29

Funeral procession for Edward VII, 1910. Rotary. R1, $5.

Funeral procession for Edward VII, 1910. Rotary. R1, $5.

Funeral of German Empress Augusta Victoria, 1921. Gustav Liersch. R4, $20

Funeral of German Empress. Unlike her husband, "Dona" was well liked and was permitted burial in Germany. Gustav Liersch. R4, $20.

| | |
|---|---|
| **1907** | Mazaffareddin of Persia, shah, January 19 |
| | Oscar II of Sweden, king, December 8 |
| **1908** | King Carlos I and Crown Prince of Portugal, February 1 (assassinated) |
| | Kwang Hgsu of China, emperor, November 14 |
| | Tsu hsi of China, dowager empress, November 15 |
| **1909** | Prince Ito of Japan, October 26 (assassinated by a Korean) |
| | Leopold II of Belgium, king, December 17 |
| **1910** | Edward VII of England, king, May 6 |
| **1912** | William IV of Luxembourg, grand duke, February 25 |
| | Frederick VIII of Denmark, king, May 15 |
| | Mutsuhito of Japan, emperor, July 29 |
| | Luitpold of Bavaria, prince regent, December 12 |
| **1913** | George I of Greece, king, March 18 (assassinated at Salonika) |
| | Prince Kataura of Japan |
| | Menelik of Abyssinia, king, December 12 (reported on December 22) |
| **1914** | Sophia of Sweden, ex-queen, January |
| | Franz Ferdinand, heir to throne of Austria-Hungary, June 28 (assassinated) |

| | |
|---|---|
| | Dowager Empress of Japan |
| | Carol I of Rumania, king, October 10 |
| **1916** | Franz Joseph of Austria-Hungary, emperor, November 21 |
| | Elisabeth of Rumania, ex-queen, March 2 |
| **1917** | Liliuokalani of Hawaii, ex-queen |
| | Hussein Kemal of Egypt, sultan |
| **1918** | Mohammed V of Turkey, sultan, July 5 |
| | Abdul Hamid, ex-sultan of Turkey |
| | Maria Theresa of Bavaria, queen |
| **1920** | Eugenie of France, ex-empress |
| | Alexander I of Greece, king |
| **1921** | Ludwig III of Bavaria, ex-king |
| | Augusta Victoria, ex-German empress |
| **1922** | Carl, ex-emperor of Austria-Hungary, April |
| **1923** | Abbas Hilmi Pasha, ex-khedive of Egypt |
| | Constantine, ex-king of Greece |
| **1924** | Marie Adelaide, ex-grande duchesse of Luxembourg, January 24 |
| **1925** | Dowager Queen Alexandra of England, November 20 |

# Marriages

Marriage of Alexander of Serbia to Draga Masin, 1900. Sepia. R5, **$30.**

Marriage of Wilhelm II's only daughter, 1913. Gustav Liersch. R3, **$15.**

Marriage of Grande Duchesse Charlotte of Luxembourg, 1919. Edward Kutter. R5, **$50.**

This is only a partial listing of some of the more important royal marriages.

1893    Crown Prince Ferdinand of Rumania, January 10
        King Ferdinand of Bulgaria, April 20
        George V (Prince of Wales), July
        William IV of Luxembourg
1894    Tsar Nicholas II of Russia, November 26
1895    Prince Haakon VII of Norway, June
1896    Crown Prince Victor Emmanuel III of Italy, October 24
1900    Crown Prince Yoshihito of Japan, May 10
        King Alexander I of Serbia
        Archduke Franz Ferdinand of Austria-Hungary, July 1
        Crown Prince Albert of Belgium

Marriage of Mary, British Princess Royale, 1922. Tuck. R3, **$10.**

1901    Queen Wilhelmina of Holland, February 7
1905    German Crown Prince Wilhelm, June 6
        Crown Prince Gustav of Sweden
1906    King Alphonso XIII of Spain, May 31
1907    Crown Prince George of Greece
1908    King Ferdinand of Bulgaria, March 1 (after death of first wife)
1910    Princess Clementine of Belgium, November 14
1911    Archduke Carl of Austria, October 21
1913    German Princess Royal Victoria, May 24
        King Manuel II of Portugal, September 4
1919    Grande Duchesse Charlotte of Luxembourg, November 6
1922    Princess Royal of England, Mary, February 28
        King Alexander of Yugoslavia, June 8
1923    George VI of England, April 26
1924    Crown Prince Hirohito of Japan, January 26

# Celebrations, Dedications, Anniversaries

One-hundredth anniversary, defeat of Napoleon, 1913. N.P.G. R3, **$15.**

Twenty-fifth wedding anniversary, King of Württenberg, 1911. Government issue. Sepia. R4, **$15.**

Twenty-fifth year of reign, Wilhelm II, 1913. R3, **$15.**

Franz Joseph, sixtieth year of reign, 1908. Sepia. R3, **$10.**

| | |
|---|---|
| **1900** | Seventieth birthday of Franz Joseph, August 18 |
| **1902** | Fiftieth year reign of Frederick of Baden, April 24 |
| **1906** | Twenty-fifth wedding anniversary of German emperor, February 27 |
| | Dedication of German Museum at Munich, November 13 |
| **1907** | German Emperor unveils memorial at Memal emblematic of rise of Prussia, September 23 |
| **1908** | Sixtieth year reign of Franz Joseph, December 2 |
| **1909** | Inauguration of statue of Alexander III in St. Petersburg |
| **1911** | Statue of Victor Emmanuel II unveiled by King of Italy, June 4 |
| | Ninetieth birthday Prince Regent Luitpold of Bavaria, March 12 |
| | Twenty-fifth wedding anniversary of Wilhelm II of Württemburg, April 8 |
| | Twenty-fifth anniversary of death of Ludwig II of Bavaria, June 13 |
| | International Exhibition of Industry opened at Turin by Italian king, April 29 |
| | German emperor unveils statue of Frederick the Great at Aix-la-Chapelle, October 18 |
| **1912** | Memorial to Queen Victoria unveiled at Cimiez, April 12 |
| | Duke of Connaught dedicates Nova Scotia Memorial, August 14 |
| | Ferdinand of Bulgaria, tsar, twenty-fifth year of reign |
| **1913** | Dedication of the Palace of Peace at The Hague, August 28 |

Dedication of World War I memorial, Crown Prince Rupprecht in attendance. R4, **$20.**

Twenty-fifth wedding anniversary Wilhelm II, 1906. Gustav Liersch. Black and white. R2, **$10.**

# Royal Visits, Miscellaneous Activities

World War I related. Inset of George V, 1914. Sepia. R1, **$5.**

George V receiving sword at Temple Bar. Valentines. Black and white. R3, **$10.**

1891    Visit of Wilhelm II and empress to Great Britain, July

Russian tsarevitch (Nicholas II) assaulted at Kyoto, Japan, May 11

1892    Meeting between German (Wilhelm II) and Russian (Alexander III) emperors at Kiel, June 7

1894    Korean Emperor appeals to China for protection against Japanese; Japanese troops occupy Seoul, June 6

Ruler of Siam (Thailand) establishes a legislative council by decree,

1895    Japanese defeat Chinese

Japanese force Chinese to recognize independence of Korea, April 7

1897    King Chulalongkorn of Siam goes on European tour

Arrival in Portsmouth, England, of King of Spain on his European tour, July 30

1898    By a coup d'etat the Dowager Empress of China assumes the regency to the virtual exclusion of Emperor Kwang-Hsu, September 21

1899    Gathering of dignitaries (Edward VII as Prince of Wales, Princess Victoria, Shah of Persia, and others) at Hatfield House, England, July 9

1900    Visit of England's Queen Victoria to Ireland at the age of eighty. While there, she was presented with the keys of Dublin by the mayor

Attempt on the life of Prince of Wales (Edward VII) by an anarchist at Brussels, April 4

1901    Russian tsar visits France and witnesses naval and army reviews, September

1902    Arrival in New York of Prince Henry of Prussia to christen the royal yacht, February 23

President Loubet of France visits Russian tsar, May 20

Prince Joachim of Prussia with fiancée, 1915. Gustav Liersch. R4, $20.

Wilhelm II at ancestor's mausoleum. AR&CB. Artist-drawn. Color. R3, $15.

**1903** Visit to France by Edward VII, May 1–4

**1905** In Paris a bomb thrown at carriage occupied by King Alphonso XIII of Spain and French President Loubet, May 7

**1906** Bomb is thrown at King and Queen of Spain after their wedding, 24 killed, royal couple unharmed, May 31

King Menelik of Abyssinia signs Franco-British-Italian treaty, August 12

Emperor of China issues edict promising a constitutional government, September 2

Emperor of China issues edict demanding eradication of opium habit in ten years, September 21

**1907** Grand dukes of Mecklenburg Schwerin and Mecklenburg Strelitz announce intention to grant constitutions to their duchies, May 4

Edward VII lays foundation stone for extension of British Museum, June 27

**1908** Austria-Hungary announces the annexation of Bosnia and Herzegovina, October 5

**1909** Crown Prince George renounces succession to the Serbian throne, March 25

The Shah of Persia grants a constitution, May 4

Greek Parliament abolishes right of royal princes to hold command in the army (October 15); it was reported that Prince George was mentally unstable, therefore this renunciation amounted to his forced removal from succession

Severe earthquake in Italy kills 200,000. King and queen view wreckage and lend assistance (1909–1910)

**1910** Prince Charles of Monaco proclaims representative government with universal suffrage, March 28

King George of Greece revises the constitution, March 30

King and Queen of Portugal flee to Gibralter after revolutionary outbreak, October 6

**1911** Emperor Wilhelm II's Society for the Promotion of Scientific Research is formally opened in Berlin, January 11

Opening at Paris of the Oceanographic Institute built by Prince of Monaco, July 23

King George V selects position for the All-India Memorial to Edward VII, December 8

Visit of French President to the Netherlands

**1912** Peace treaty between Italy and Turkey signed at Ouchy, Switzerland, October 18

**1913** Universal Peace Conference convened at The Hague, August 20

Greece and Turkey sign peace treaty at Athens, November 5

**1914** Serbia and Turkey sign peace treaty at Constantinople, March 14

Visit of George V to France, April

Kaiser Wilhelm II's War Council at Potsdam, July 5

**1921** Prince Hirohito of Japan visits Western Europe, June

Another area of postcard announcement centered around the birth of royal infants. While it is not possible to be categoric about the rarity of these in a complete way, it is no matter of speculation that all are at least scarce. As a general rule, the birth cards of Western European royalty (except those prior to 1898) are the least difficult to acquire (R2–R3), while those from Eastern Europe are less easily obtained (R3–R4). The real challenge is finding specimens from the other royal families of the world (R4–R5). Few from this last group are seen more than very infrequently. They are never routinely offered, even by dealers specializing in desirable and seldom-seen material.

Royal birth cards are often overlooked, and that is to the collector's detriment. Pictures of royal infants have the beneficial effect of raising the progeny from the obscurity of history texts and genealogical charts. With the postcard's aid, one is able to see them for what they were, flesh and blood children whose appearance was occasion for parental happiness and presumed proof of the continuation of the monarchical tradition.

World War I related. Inset of King Albert, 1914. Sepia. R1, **$5.**

Funeral of Franz Joseph, 1916. Black and white. R4, **$20.**

The many faces of "Mad" Ludwig. Sepia. R2, **$10.**

Festival for Franz Joseph, 1908. R4, **$20.**

Prussian Prince Eitel Friedrich with his fiancée. Gustav Liersch. R4, **$20.**

Carl's triumphal ride through Budapest as King of Hungary, 1916. R5, **$35.**

King and Queen of Portugal attending church services, 1901.
Sepia.  R3, **$15.**

Festival for Franz Joseph, 1908.  Photochemie.  R3, **$15.**

Luxembourg and Belgian royalty, 1922.  R5, **$30.**

Wilhelm II visiting Reichstag, 1917.  Black and white.  R3, **$15.**

King of Italy on state visit to Paris, 1903.  L.L.  Black and white.
R3, **$15.**

George V visiting grave of nurse Edith Cavell.  Black and white.
R3, **$15.**

King Ferdinand of Bulgaria with the war effort, 1916. Artist-drawn, Black and white. R4, **$20.**

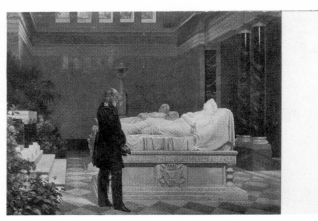

Wilhelm I visiting ancestors. E.A. Seemann. Artist-drawn. Color. R2, **$10.**

Wilhelm II and Edward VII: Uncle and nephew. Each disliked and mistrusted the other. Davidson Brothers. Sepia. R5, **$25.**

King Constantine of Greece reviewing his troops. Black and white. R3, **$15.**

Wilhelm II landing in England in happier days, 1907. Rotophot. R4, **$15.**

Granada surrendered to King and Queen of Spain, 1492. Artist-drawn. Color. R2, **$10.**

Italy's leaders during World War I. Sepia.
R3, **$15.**

Wedding of German crown prince, 1905.
Sepia. R3, **$15.**

Twenty-fifth year reign, Wilhelm II, 1913.
N.P.G. R3, **$15.**

Twenty-fifth year reign, Wilhelm II, 1913.
Photochemie. R3, **$15.**

Photograph for Hospital Fund of George
V. R3, **$10.**

Italian-Turkish peace treaty, 1912. Sepia.
R3, **$15.**

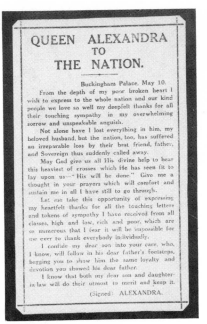

Queen Alexandra's address to the nation following the death of Edward VII. R1, **$5.**

Twenty-fifth anniversary reign, Ferdinand of Bulgaria, 1912. Government issue. Sepia/purple. R3, **$15.**

Queen Victoria, "The Grandmother of Europe." Memorial card. Wrench. R3, **$15.**

Mourning card for Edward VII, 1910. S. Newcomb and Company. Black and white. R3, **$15.**

Twenty-fifth year of regency, Luitpold of Bavaria, 1911. Artist-drawn, Sepia. R3, **$10.**

Opening of the German Museum in Munich, 1906. Becker & Kolblinger. Sepia. R3, **$15.**

Sixtieth year reign, Franz Joseph, 1908.
Lederer & Popper. Sepia. R3, **$15.**

Fiftieth year reign, Friedrich of Baden,
1902. Frederick Spies. R4, **$20.**

Christening of Princess Juliana, Holland,
1909. Sepia. R3, **$10.**

Souvenir of Carl's coronation as King of
Hungary, 1916. Sepia. R3, **$15.**

Souvenir of King of Hungary's coronation,
1916. This is Zita, Carl's wife. R3, **$15.**

Marriage of Wilhelm II's only daughter,
1913. Gustav Liersch. R3, **$15.**

Inauguration ceremonies, Grande Duchesse of Luxembourg, 1912. R5, **$35.**

Dutch royal infant with Queen and Prince Consort, 1909. Rotophot. R2. **$5.**

Anglo-French unity, World War I, Color. R2, **$10.**

Crown Prince Rudolph of Austria and his mistress. Both were reported to have committed suicide. Black and white. R2, **$10.**

Regent Horthy entering Budapest, 1919. Although Horthy was supposed to have dispensed with royalty, his own title was "Your Highness." R5, **$35.**

Memorial card, dowager Queen Alexandra. The queen is seen here with one of many animals she befriended during her lifetime. Tuck. R3, **$10.**

German Empress encouraging the troops. N.P.G. R4, **$20.**

Prince Luitpold of Bavaria, postmarked on date of death, 1912. R4, **$20.**

German and Austrian royalty and military. WRB & Co. Sepia. R3, **$15.**

Edward VII and Queen Alexandra on parade. R3, **$15.**

# 6

# Categories of Interest

**Relaxing Royalty.** Like most folk, royal personages enjoyed finding an occasion to take time from the daily routine and relax. The activities that constituted their vacations and relaxations were as diverse as the people themselves. For the business-oriented Franz Joseph, this often meant either a hiking expedition or a grouse hunt. More rarely, it might include a trip to the beautiful Opera House at Vienna with a young female companion named Katarina Schratt. The slightly plump Schratt, a sometime actress and opera performer, was neither the emperor's mistress nor even a frequent companion. Franz was much too busy with state business to devote appreciable time to anyone. There is considerable evidence that Empress Elisabeth, plagued by guilt over her continued absence and lack of attention to the emperor, had introduced Schratt to Franz Joseph herself. In any event, although the aged monarch was certainly fond of the young lady (while she herself became the butt of not a few nasty one-liners and limericks), his main energies were focused elsewhere, and his romantic ties remained always with Elisabeth.

As with Austria's ruler, so it was with many other monarchs. Although England produced a playboy in the person of Edward VII and Spain had its hands full keeping up with the extracurricular activities of Alphonso XIII, most royal leaders were rather tame and pedestrian in their pursuit of leisure. Even Germany's Wilhelm II, notwithstanding his reckless abandon at the English regattas and the notorious boar and stag hunts that so amused him, felt most at ease aboard the royal yacht anchored at Kiel or knee-deep in dirt at an archaeological site. In quieter moments, this otherwise boisterous Kaiser also considered himself a composer and painter.

Marble boat at summer palace. Chinese royal splendor. Kingshill Trading Company. Sepia. R1, $5.

Italy's Victor Emmanuel III sought pleasure in family outings, on photographic excursions, or in adding a rare specimen to his renowned coin collection. To the ill-fated Franz Ferdinand, nothing in life held as much contentment as a quiet evening at home with his morganatic wife and their children. Bavaria counted among members of its royal house a doctor who spent his free hours gathering botanical specimens. Out of military cloth, away from military maneuvers, and free from the political spotlight, many were almost boringly peaceful. Looking at them, revelling, dabbling, or perhaps contendedly reading a newspaper or enjoying a cup of tea, it seems difficult to imagine the extent to which the political and social fortunes of mankind were entwined in their persons.

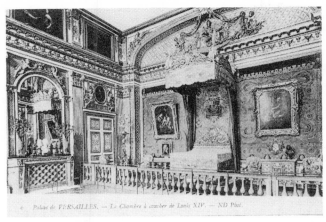

The incomparable palace at Versailles. N.D. Phot. Color. R1, $2.

Another view of Versailles. Color. R1, $2.

**Royal Ridicule.** "Will Hell Have Him?" the postcard asks in an obvious twisting of letters to remind the viewer of Germany's Wilhelm II. So that the point is driven with sufficient force, a drawing of the kaiser with an oversized version of the insolently upturned moustache is rendered below. Not the first, and certainly far from the last, this postcard is only one from a large group of unflattering royal caricatures.

The actual date that the first royal caricature postcard was created is unknown. What is known is that few of the world's heads of state between the years 1888 to 1919 escaped such characterizations. Whether these drawings were intended as political propaganda or as attempts to give the high and mighty comeuppance is a question not often asked by the modern collector of postcards, who usually prefers to see the humor or recognize the slander and ridicule as qualities unto themselves.

But for the people who lived through those years of changing political climates and fortunes, the cards served as harbingers of very significant events. And none of the messages was quite so important as the unwritten implication that many of the people being lampooned were either menaces or incompetents that the human race would be better off without. Wilhelm II and Franz Joseph were the most frequently portrayed as mankind's chief offenders, so it is small wonder that there are countless cards devoted to each. Their connection to World War I was viewed with a rousing condemnation from almost every corner of the globe outside their respective empires. But Germany and Austria were postcard manufacturing countries as well, and both produced a quantity of unsavory material relating to their "brothers of the purple" from the opposing side.

The clock could actually be turned back to the period before that first great international conflict, since ridiculing royalty had been a favorite pastime of political cartoonists for many years prior to 1914. As long as the artist had the good sense to remain a safe distance from the object of his derision, there was never any fear that his art would be decommissioned or that his lampooning would not find a receptive audience.

Of special merit and mention are the cards drawn by the caricaturists Rostro and Orens. Both men loved deflating the egos of world leaders and making them appear more ridiculous than the common man. No doubt their primary intention was to let their "betters" realize that the role of kingship in the twentieth century was supposed to be one of service and dedication rather than one of aloof condescension. Rostro and Orens may not have achieved this goal but their amusing drawings undeniably blasted some of the stuffier royal characters with discomfort and gave the viewing public a chance to examine the institution of monarchy from refreshingly uncommon perspectives.

As might be expected, however, the greatest period of output for the caricaturist came during World War I, a time when he could give fee reign to his scathing pictorial comment. The vast array of types and the immense numbers of these cards being offered for sale today indicate that the artists had a field day at the expense of the exalted ones. As tools of propaganda, the cards were of incomparable value. The perception of the enemy rulers' proclivity to viciousness, warmongering, and immoral behavior was ingrained in populations where nationalistic fervor went hand in hand with hatred of an enemy country's leader. The postcard exacerbated, then continued to feed, these feelings with half comical, half ghastly depictions. To the Allies (France, England, Belgium, and others, including after 1917, the United States), Kaiser Wilhelm, Franz Joseph, or Tsar Ferdinand were representative of everything evil and depraved in human nature. The Central Powers (Germany, Austria-Hungary, Bulgaria, and Turkey) viewed George V, Nicholas II, and even the intellectual and soft-tempered Woodrow Wilson as the souls and visible manifestations of corruption and debauchery.

But humor was also in abundance, and many of the artistic renditions were crackling with gibes at monarchs that elicited a guffaw even as the allegory or satire gave the viewer pause for political reflection. Better than any history book, these postcards tell us much about the feelings, anxieties, and mind-sets of our forefathers' generation of people.

Royal Palace, The Hague, with occupants in insets. Beagles. R2, $5.

The royal castle, Stockholm, Sweden. Svenska Amerikanaren. Color. R1, $5.

**Royalty in Repose.** One might be tempted, when considering the accolades that are often showered over the dead bodies of deceased monarchs, to conclude: As in life, so in death. They are treated well in life and well thought of after it.

For the most part, these statements are substantial and accurate. What they omit is that reflection, like the proverbial fish story, has a tendency to make the event, person, or thing greater than the reality. A two-pound fish will grow in time and memory to twice that size. The simple expedient of death imparts a significance (either good or ill) to royal personages that often magnifies their real life deeds and personalities. It makes one wonder if hindsight is always as perfect as it is presumed to be.

The curiosity about their life-styles, their deeds, and misdeeds, the sometime mystery surrounding their comings and goings; all assume the flavor of a savory soup, once tasted and relished, now only faintly remembered. And like that food, which both loses and gains by memory and conversation, the lives of royal figures after their deaths are ever subject to reinterpretation. Was Edward VII really such a rogue? Was Wilhelm II the true originator of World War I or was he led to it by forces and people known and unknown? Did Queen Victoria always wear black after Albert's death? Even in privacy?

And always and always the questions. Fuel for gossip, fodder to be examined, trampled upon, re-examined.

Postcard producers didn't care to answer the questions, but they did welcome the consumer's demand for card after card of funerals, statues, and memorials of every description. Most were rather mundane, ordinary prints and photographs. Not all, however. Some, in fact a goodly number, were embossed, hand-colored, and embellished with diverse designs in such ways as to make them more attractive.

Varnishing the uncertain portrait and polishing it to a brilliant sheen, they created cards not for the benefit of the deceased monarch, but rather as tributes to the living memory of him.

**Royal Residences.** One of the chief interests of royalty watchers has been a curiosity about royal residences. Whether they be castles, villas, or mansions, the designation is of less importance than the actual seeing of what the place looked like. And if the view was of the interior, so much the better. Postcard publishers, quick to catch the drift of popular sentiment, catered to the public appetite for views of their majesties' homes. Balmoral in Scotland (Queen Victoria's favorite residence); the Royal Castle in Copenhagen; schlosses all over Germany; boudoirs, audience chambers, billiard rooms; all were fair game for photographers and artists.

The most popular view, and one that postcard firms still capture on pasteboard, is the Palace at Versailles. Inside, outside, lawns, gardens, fountains, even views of the rear have been overdone to the point of distraction. In truth, publishers can hardly be blamed for this, because no other royal residence in the world can begin to compare to Versailles in splendor or aesthetics.

On the other hand, it must be admitted that some royal habitations were less than awe-inspiring. A few, like those in Serbia and Montenegro, had exteriors that might be termed shabby, in comparison to an upper middle-class home in today's Western World. But in their place and in their time they were seen as splendid and ranking as the best the given nation could afford.

One of the more interesting set of cards in this category is entitled "The Queen's Dollhouses." Composed of forty-eight cards, the set depicts English royal homes reproduced in what was reputed to be exact miniature renderings. Somewhat on the expensive side when purchased as a complete set, they are certainly worth a stop at a dealer's table to examine. Particular attention should be paid to the furniture settings and decorations. They often reveal surprising similarities between royalty and folk with humbler pretensions.

Of course there was and is a large difference. While many people decorate and furnish their homes in royal style, the results never achieve the aura of majesty and

Lord Darnley's Room, Holyrood. Sepia. R1, **$2.**

Tower of London, The Regalia. London Stereoscopic Company. Sepia. R1, **$2.**

mystery that is exclusively royal. There is no escaping the truth that behind palace doors lives a special person or family that stands apart and lives a different life.

**Unusual Royal Cards.** As postcard producers started increasing their volume of business during the years 1897 to 1914, they also began to experience the threat of competition. This necessitated the exploration of new techniques and gimmicks to keep the buying public interested in their wares. Some of these original ideas became accepted staples, while others quickly languished. What many publishers failed to realize, was that necessity was the same "mother of invention" for their competitors as it was for themselves. Like the automobile makers of today who copy the innovations of the competition, producers of picture postcards were only too willing to "borrow" the ideas of their brothers in the trade while promoting an idea of their own from time to time.

The result of this scramble to get to or remain at the top of the sales heap, was a never-ending stream of postcard types to delight or amuse the buying public. Even in those days people were aware that these novelties had artistic and inventive merit. They were saved in large numbers for what was thought to be future generations of avid postcard collectors.

As is well known, disillusionment with the political and social order that existed prior to 1914 caused people in the 1920s to discard reminders of earlier times. A new literature, disenchanted and pessimistic in tone, plus new styles in art and architecture that deviated as far as possible from the past, and a new view of the common man and his place in the universe all aimed to erase remaining vestiges of old days and old ways. This discarding—nice play on words—applied to the humble postcard also, and none were pitched with more relish than those of royalty. Literally dethroned, their figurative representations on paperboard soon followed them.

By the time countless attics had been cleaned (not to mention the untold thousands of albums that were consigned to the dustbin), what was once an overabundance of unusual royal cards was reduced to a smidgen. The mighty river of material had become a small stream into which the collectors of 1960s and 1970s hurled their nets in order to salvage a few remaining treasures. Now, even though thousands of specimens are still extant, demand far exceeds the supply. Some are more easily found than others, but pricetags for all are commensurate with rarity and desirability.

A list of unusual royal cards will include the following types:

**Embossed coin cards.** Either depict the ruler on replicas of coins or display a portrait alongside the coin reproduction on the picture side of card.

**Embossed stamp cards.** As above with stamp reproductions instead of coins.

**Metamorphics.** Busts of various rulers with classical motifs of nude women or military figures.

**Bas-relief.** Pictures of rulers, alone or with family members, which are raised from the surface of the card to create a three-dimensional effect.

**Clay or wax model cards.** Representations of various rulers as musicians, tradespeople, or posed in generally ridiculous situations.

**Installment cards.** Separate cards that fit together to depict a ruler, often with illustrations allegorical or actual events pertinent to that person.

**Insect cards.** Show the face of a monarch with the body of an insect. Were popular during World War I. The Allies were usually depicted as butterflies, while the Central Powers were shown as troublesome and irritating creatures (bees, wasps, etc.).

The tomb of Napoleon. Color. R1, *$2.*

Wilhelm II at a lawn party. N.P.G. R4, *$20.*

Edward VII and Alexandra on a drive. Rotophot. R3, *$15.*

Wilhelm II and German Empress visiting a school. Gustav Liersch. R4, *$20.*

**Playing cards.** Depict the monarch (and occasionally a consort) as one of the face cards or even the ace in a deck of playing cards.

**Cellophane see-throughs.** On these, the royal personage is "hidden" behind a cellophane window.

**Puzzle cards.** Turned to the right and left—or upside-down, these reveal an outline or a second presence.

**Ruler insets.** Embossed ovals with a royal person inside. Above is a crown. Usually heavy paperboard.

**Advertising cards.** Show the monarch sampling the product being advertised or alone on the picture side with advertising on the back.

**Cards with attachments or material.** Decorative additions to the card's surface.

**Flag cards.** Several types fall into this category. The most commonly encountered depict the ruler in an oval inset with a national flag in the background.

**Fold-outs.** Two, three, or four cards folded together.

**Royalty booklets.** Detachable cards in a booklet. Usually black and white or sepia.

**Hidden door.** Have compartments that, when opened, release folded pictures of royal family members and residences.

**Song and flag cards.** Usually these have an embossed oval into which a photograph of the ruler is placed. At the top are a few musical notes of the national hymn. The card itself is often printed in the colors of the national flag.

**Mechanicals.** The movement may reveal either the monarch at various stages of his life or picture him with various family members. May occasionally portray the ruler as a figure of ridicule or humor.

**Woven silk and fabric patchwork.** Image of the monarch or royal figure is woven in pure silk or applied to a cushioned, satin or silk surface.

Haakon VII of Norway on a carriage ride. R2, **$10.**

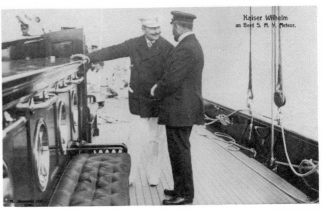

Wilhelm II on board his yacht *Meteor.* Gustav Liersch. R3, **$15.**

German Empress, her daughter, and the Duchess of Cumberland. Gustav Liersch. R3, **$15.**

Queen Elisabeth of Belgium with wife of French president. R4, **$20.**

Stamp card, Luxembourg. Ottmar Zieher. Embossed. Color. R4, **$15.**

German Empress visiting war victims during World War I. R3, **$15.**

German Crown Prince. Gustav Liersch. R3, **$10.**

German Crown Prince "Little Willy." Gustav Liersch. Sepia. R3, **$15.**

The Round Tower, Windsor Castle. Peacock Brand. Sepia. R1, **$2.**

Monument to Kaiser Karl in Frankfurt. Sepia. R1, **$2.**

Monument of Saigo in Tokyo. Color. R1, **$5.**

Bust of German Emperor Friedrich III, a man of ideals. Black and white. R2, **$10.**

The final resting place of Austrian emperors. R1, **$2.**

Eccentric, high-strung Empress Elisabeth of Austria. Color. R1, **$5.**

World War I caricature of Wilhelm II. Black and white. R3, **$15.**

American view of Wilhelm II during World War I. Lightly colored. R3, **$15.**

Russian bear trees the kaiser. Lawrence and Jellicoe. Color. R3, **$15.**

Equestrian monument to Italy's Victor Emmanuel. Browntone. R1, **$2.**

German Empress with the Crown Princess, her daughter-in-law. Gustav Liersch. R3, **$10.**

Austrian Emperor Carl with two of his children, taken in exile. Black and white. R4, **$20.**

The kaiser proving his manhood. N.P.G. R4, **$15.**

Prince August Wilhelm of Prussia. N.P.G. R2, **$10.**

Victor Emmanuel III and Queen Elena. R3, **$15.**

Metamorphic. Abdul Hamid of Turkey. Black and white. R4, **$20.**

Another metamorphic of Abdul Hamid. Black and white. R4, **$20.**

Metamorphic, Napoleon. Face and head-gear composed of soldiers. Black and white. R4, **$20.**

Prince of Wales, bas-relief. George V. Warwick Brothers. R2, **$10.**

Queen Alexandra, bas-relief. Beagles. R2, **$10.**

Edward VII, bas-relief. Taber. Tinted with sparkles added. R2, **$10.**

Bas-relief, Princess of Wales. Taber. R2, $10.

Spain's Alphonso XIII. Color. R3, $10.

Kaiser as dedicated military leader. Color. R3, $15.

Wilhelm II and Crown Prince at the latter's headquarters. Like father, like son? N.P.G. R4, $20.

Kaiser Wilhelm II in less worrisome, harmful days. Arthur Rehn. Sepia. R3, $15.

Kaiser as protector of the crown. A humorous card not meant to be humorous. Sepia. R3, $15.

Italy's Crown Prince Humbert hiking. R3, $15.

Prince Eugen of Austria. Color. R3, $10.

Wilhelm II in admiral's uniform. Tuck Oilette. Color. R3, $10.

Prince Eugen of Austria. Color. R3, $15.

Emperor Carl of Austria-Hungary. Red Cross card, Color. R3, $15.

Luxembourg's William IV. Bernhoeft. Sepia. R4, $20.

Prince Frederich of Austria. Von Christoph Sohne. Color. R3, **$15.**

Princesses Louisa and Monica of Saxony. Gustav Schmidt. R4, **$20.**

Germany's Warlord. Gustav Liersch. Sepia. R3, **$10.**

Marriage announcement, Clementine of Belgium and Prince Victor Napoleon of the House of Bonaparte. Sepia. R4, **$20.**

German Empress in a fashionably outsized hat. Unlike her husband, it did not match her ego. N.P.G. R3, **$15.**

Only daughter of Wilhelm II. R3, **$15.**

Ernst August, only son-in-law of Wilhelm II. Gustav Liersch. R4, **$15.**

Silhouette of German Empress. Gustav Liersch. R3, **$10.**

Silhouette of Wilhelm II. Gustav Liersch. R3, **$10.**

King Friedrich August of Saxony. Photochemie. R3, **$15.**

Cecilie, German Crown Princess. Yellow tone. R3, **$15.**

# 7

# Artist-Drawn and Royalty-Signed Cards

Two categories of royal postcards that are now undervalued in the world market will be dealt with in this chapter. A lack of appreciation among many dealers for both the artist-drawn and the royalty-signed cards has created an opportunity for the astute collector to gather specimens before the prices inevitably rise.

Regarding the artist-drawn card, conventional thinking suggests that since there is a relatively ample supply of them, they should be priced according to available numbers. But this thinking falls into error insofar as it neglects a crucial element. Dealers are correct in supposing that there are many extant specimens of this type, but they are incorrect in believing that there are countless numbers of each particular card. While it is obviously true that there are dozens if not hundreds of Artist-drawn cards of Wilhelm II and Franz Joseph (to name two who represent a sizable portion of this category), it is equally true that, with few exceptions, the individual cards do not exist in anything approaching infinite quantity. In other words one may obtain a particular card without much trouble, but finding a second card like the first is less easily accomplished, and finding a third may prove highly difficult.

The argument that frequently follows, once this assertion is tested and accepted, states that one artist-drawn card of Wilhelm II (or Franz Joseph, Edward VII, et al) is much like another. Why bother with two cards that resemble one another so closely? This naive sort of thinking is almost too ludicrous to be given credence. Would any dealer—or collector—who presumed to know anything about postcards say that one card of a special event is like another card of the same event? Clearly not.

In the case of Artist-drawn royal cards, each could represent a different artist, or a different pose, or a different uniform, or a different setting, or a different rationale for its existence, and so forth. And even all these differences omit the fact that not all these cards are equally well done or artistically rendered.

For many of the same reasons, the facile arguments about the pricing of royalty-signed cards (reference here is being made to facsimile signatures, since authentic ones are obviously worth multiples of the stamped signature material) may be just as routinely discounted. In addition, one should always be aware that handwriting is subject to alteration according to circumstances and situations. This is frequently evidenced in the handwriting of Wilhelm II. Before World War I most of his signature examples displayed a boldness and originality. At the outbreak of the war the flourishes and embellishments were even more pronounced. However, as the conflict continued and Germany's situation worsened, the kaiser's handwriting became poorer in quality, and in some instances it was little more than a scrawl. The value of these later signatures would be of immeasurable worth to psychologists, graphologists, and to postcard collectors with a historical orientation.

What is true of Wilhelm is also applicable to other world leaders. Combine this component with the realization that many world royalty signatures, even the facsimile types, are rarely seen, and the value of them comes into bolder focus.

A last comment regarding the artist-drawn card concerns their artistic merit. Although some of them were merely reproductions of existing paintings, many others were originals. After seventy years, they have also assumed the rightful title of antiques. Placed in an appropriate frame with good matting board, they could rival much of what passes for "art" in some middle class homes these days.

The list of postcard artists, a rather lengthy one, includes names that range from the famous and popular to the obscure. The more commonly recognized are the following. Asterisks placed after certain artists' names indicate those most sought after.

| | | |
|---|---|---|
| Bauer, Karl | Fischer, Art* | Pietzner |
| Bieber, B. | Forster, E. | Ravenny, L. |
| Benesch, C.* | Franken, B.* | Renatus, O.* |
| Berger, Georg | Grieger, W. | Rostro* |
| Bruch, O.* | Growald, Martin* | Schneider, Rud. |
| Bruncher | Hornert, S.* | Schodde, W. |
| Carcedo, P. | Kalous, J. | Scoliksen, Charles |
| Dreger, T. | Kaskeline* | Schwormstadt |
| Dussek, Edward | Klamroth, Hofrat | Snowman, I.* |
| Dulst, J. | Lafayette | Thomas, Bert* |
| Ehrlich, Felix* | Lehmann* | Ulmer, H. |
| Fasche, Theo. | Orens* | Van Der Hern, Piet |
| Ferraris, Arthur | Pape, Wilh.* | Wall* |
| Firle, Walther | Payne, Harry* | Wiedemann, Otto |
| | | Wilda, H.G. |

# 8

# Postcard Publishers

From the late 1890s to the early years of the 1920s the picture postcard industry was experiencing its most robust period of growth and diversity. Although the years following 1914 saw a gradual decline, there was still a great deal of collecting and producing activity to be seen. Publishing firms came into existence by the dozens and, while some did significantly more business than others, all were bustling with activity as they competed to fill the ever-growing demands of a postcard crazed public.

As might be expected, not all postcard publishers met with equal success. The more established firms that were already involved with printing other kinds of paper items quickly came to the fore and established dominance in the new industry. Inevitably the smaller entrepreneurs with less sophisticated equipment, fewer photographers and artists on the payroll and less capital, were squeezed out of the field by their stronger competitors. But though gone, they are not forgotten, because many of their specimens survive to this day as testimonies to their contributions and their ingenuity.

As for those who remained and prospered it would be safe to assume that they did so for two primary reasons: They were able to meet and satisfy public tastes; and, in the case of truly inventive publishers, were able to introduce new styles and concepts into postcard manufacture with consistently successful results.

It was due to the imaginations of these firms that the modern collector may possess such beauties as woven silk cards or items of wonder like mechanicals, metamorphics, hold-to-lights, bas-reliefs, and cellophane transparencies. Such oddities as cards made of wood, cards with attachments, and cards that emit sounds when pressed add further dimension to modern collecting.

It should be noted that the publisher of a postcard and the printer of it were not always one and the same. In many cases the publisher, who might be anyone from the corner druggist to a painter or photographer with a keen eye for detail, was merely the seller of the finished product. The production and printing were entrusted to firms with the necessary expertise to render the idea and original material into a purchasable item.

More often than not, German companies were selected because of their superior technology. With their ready access to beautifully colored inks, their master craftsmen skilled in fine lithography, and their high-quality, German-made presses, they quickly took and maintained the lead in postcard production. Even some of the larger publishers were not averse to sending their photographs and artwork to German firms, secure in the knowledge that what they would receive in return was a postcard of exquisite beauty. Collectors of postcards can be thankful for this, since the cards produced by these firms are nothing less than miniature masterpieces.

The list of postcard producers and publishers is a full one. And, until some fearless soul steps forward, after years of research, with what might purport to be a total list of them all, it will remain incomplete. In the meantime, certain names should not go unmentioned. The following number among the most well-known, prolific, and admired in the field. (More details about specific offerings are given in the chapter on Sets and Series.)

**Gustav Liersch and Co.** Most postcard collectors might think that the largest single producer of royal postcards was the well-known international firm of Raphael Tuck. Told that this was erroneous, they would probably go on to name such prestigious publishers as Valentines or the Rotary Company. A passing salute might even be made to the equally prominent Davidson Brothers. All these would be good nominations, but all are incorrect. The largest producer, and by a sizable margin, was the German firm of Gustav Liersch. Confining itself almost exclusively to German and Austrian nobility, Liersch and Company printed literally thousands of individual cards in the years spanning from the late 1890s to the 1920s. The bulk of Liersch's material was from strikingly reproduced photographs. The images are usually so clear and detailed that the viewer develops a sense of immediacy about them, almost as if he or she were standing beside the photographer when the picture was taken. Liersch's work, even with sepia-toned cards, is unsurpassed in this area. Part of the appeal of Liersch's cards is in the fact that the photographs were not retouched but went directly from negative to engraver to press. This historically accurate reproduction makes his cards much sought after. Although large numbers of Liersch cards were produced, they are not as easy to find in quantity as might be supposed.

**Raphael Tuck.** Undoubtedly the most well known of all postcard producers is Raphael Tuck. Generally speaking, most of Tuck's work is commendable. Nor is the firm to be faulted for producing and offering some material that was subpar and second rate. Like Aristotle taking the whole world of knowledge for his province and thereby occasionally falling into error, Tuck entered the postcard business like a rushing wind and swept into virtually every category imaginable. They fell short of perfection from time to time, but it is equally true that they often set the standard and made the prototypes for other firms. Originally granted a royal patent from Queen Victoria, Tuck produced, among their various offerings, many royal postcards, and some were of exceptional quality. Whether of coronations, deaths, marriages, or family groupings, the firm produced cards of nearly every type. To the collector of British royalty material, the name Raphael Tuck is as familiar as Gustav Liersch, Rotophot, and N.P.G. are to collectors of German cards. However, unlike Liersch, Tuck ranged far afield, leaving a legacy of cards of monarchs from the world over.

**Stengel Art Co.** With the exception of Raphael Tuck, no other postcard producer offered as much variety in their work as the Stengel Art Company. From crude pencil renditions, to black and white photographs, to breathtakingly beautiful mini-paintings, Stengel presented the world with a full spectrum of postcard possibilities. Their finest offerings were the colorful royal postcards, and their 29,000 series of rulers and their consorts is often thought to encompass the most gorgeous cards ever printed. Words are inadequate to describe the appeal that these cards have for viewers. Unfortunately all of Stengels' work in the field of royalty was not as well done as these. But to the firm's credit, none of the cards sink to the level of being ordinary. In addition, Stengel's early start in the 1890s furnishes the royal card collector with some views of nobility he might not otherwise have.

**N.P.G.** Almost on a numeric par with Liersch, this German publisher operated both independently and in conjunction with other producers such as E. Bieber and Liersch. In many cases it is obvious that companies other than N.P.G. printed the cards that bear its numbers. But since the numbers are attached to the N.P.G. identification, the company must be viewed as at least a publisher. Like Liersch their output was prodigious and most of it was in the area of real photograph cards, although there are notable exceptions.

**L.L.** Frequently identified as a photographer rather than producer, the enigmatic Frenchman known as L.L., was linked with at least two separate publishing firms. There is some evidence to support the claim that L.L. might have self-published as well. These initials seen on view cards that traverse the distance from Western Europe to the Far East tell of a world traveler who always had his (or her) camera ready. For some inexplicable reason, L.L. numbered some cards but not others. We might not know the rationale for this, but we may be grateful that, numbered or unnumbered, there are many royal cards—including a few very early ones—among L.L.'s massive output.

**Franz Huld.** Generally recognized in connection with a number of early American view cards, Huld published at least four cards (255 through 258) related to the visit of Prince Henry (brother of Wilhelm II) to the United States on board the North German steamship, *Kronprinz Wilhelm,* February 1902. The royal yacht, *The Hohenzollern,* was also brought along and christened in U.S. waters by Alice Roosevelt, daughter of the president. Joseph Koehler, a New York publisher, produced a few cards for the event (No. 65 and at least one more, unnumbered), as did Koelling and Klappenback of Chicago (Nos. 22 and 29) and Edward Buttner and Company of Berlin.

Of course, there are many other prominent publishing firms. Many are dealt with in the chapter that follows. This list includes the publishers whose credentials in the field of royal postcards are unquestioned. A few will have special notations where deemed appropriate, although all are deserving of special attention.

A.N.
A.P.
AR & CB
Aktiebolags
F. H. Altman
American Italian General Relief Committee
    (Issued cards for the relief of victims of the earthquake
    at Messina, Italy, 1908. Each card numbered in bold
    type on front. At least 150,000 printed.)
Svenska Americanaren
B. Angerstein
Aristophot
J. I. Austen

B.H.C.
B.K.W.I.
B.L.

Ballerini and Fratini
Bamforth and Company
J. Beagles and Company
Bernhoeft
Beger and Rockel
E. Bieber
Birn Brothers
Blankwaardt and Schoohoven
Bohn, Jos. Paul
Bouchetal, G.
Bruning, Aug.
Brunotte, A and H
Buttner, Edward and Co.

C.L.C.
Cailliau, G.
Central Sales Bureau
Cinema Art Ltd.

D.R.M.G.
Daily Mail
Davidson Brothers
Deek, H.C.J.
de Haan, W.
den Boer, W.
de Zimmerauer, H.
Dobrecourt, H. M.
Dutta

E.B. and C.
E.P. and Company
ELD
Eliasson, Axel
Eneret
Engel, Adolph
Ettlinger

Facler, M.
Faulkner, C.W.
Fink, Albert
Finke
FOW, Walter

G.D. and D.L.
G.G. Company
G.G.J.
G.H.Z.
Gale and Polden
Goldiner, J.
Grant
Grober, Friedrich
Guggenheim and Company

H. + St
H.S.I.B.
H.S.M.
Hatton, J.G.
Hauser and Menet
Haustraas, P.
Hein, Percy
Herpich, Martin
Heuchkel, Fritz
Hildebrandt, A.
Holloway's Pills and Ointment
Homann, Sussane
Hummel, Franz

Imberg and Lefson
Island Curio Store
Kingshill
Klement, L.
Knackstedt and Company
Kohn, Bruder
Kutter, Edward

L and P
Langley and Sons, Ltd.
Lautz & Isenbeck
Leconte, A.
Lederer and Popper
Lehmann, J.F.
Lemaitre
Liga, O.K.
Livingston, Arthur
London Stereoscopic Series
Lowy, J.

M.C.I.B.
M.H.B.
M.L.M.
Mansel
Mahler, P.
Manien
Meissner and Buch
Menke-Huber
Menet, Hauser Y.
Modlano, G.
Molfese, Eliotipia
Moos, Geschwister
Munk, M.

N.D.
N.F.G.
N.R.M.
Neli, Ed

Newcomb, S & Company
New Haven Illustrating Company
   (Popular World War I propaganda set. Most well-known
   ones include: picture of cracked egg that reveals out-
   line of Wilhelm II (title: "A Bad Egg"); and Kaiser with
   his feet soaking watches a U.S. soldier passing by (title:
   "Kaiser Smells the Feet," i.e. defeat.)
O.P.F.

P.F.B.
Papeghin, A.
Philco Publishing
Photochemie
Photochrome
Pictorial Newspaper Company
Piek
Punch

R.L. and K.
Rapid Photo Company
Realty
Rehn, Arthur and Sons
Reichard and Lindner
Reissers (Sohne), Christoph
Rotary
Rotograph
Rotophot A.G.
Ruitenbeek, B.
J. Russell and Sons

S.I.P.
S.V.D.
Samuels, J.J.
Saulsohn, S. and G.
Schaefers, J.H.
Scherl, August
Schmidt, Gustav
Schuler, Ernst
Schwerdtieger, E.A.
Scopes and Company Ltd.
Sfetea, C.
Sharpe, W.N.
Souvenir Company
Spielman, H.S.
Spies, Friedrich
Stender
Stewart and Woolf

Taber
Taylor, A. and G.
Thill, Ern.
Tokyo Printing Company

Traldi, A.
Trenkler, Dr. and Company
Tulate

U.S.A. Postcard
Uitgave Nijgh and Van Ditman
Underwood and Underwood
Valentine's
Wald, Jacob
Warwick Brothers
Wassman, Wilhelm
Wilkinson, E.H. & Co., Ltd.
Wrench, J.E.
Young, A.J.
Zieher, Otto

# 9
# Sets and Series

Numbers, numbers, numbers. These are encountered on postcard after postcard, regardless of topic. Nor are royal postcards any exception, as there are sets and series beyond counting and cataloging. Complicating the matter further is the fact that one cannot always tell what the number represents. Was it for a legitimate set or for a series? Was it a point of reference for the photographer, the printer, or for the publisher?

Thankfully, much of the mystery was removed by the publishers themselves in an effort to keep the public interested in their next offerings. And even in those instances where questions remain, the application of a number is regarded as immeasurably helpful to those collectors attempting to impose some numeric order on their cards. Oftentimes it is easy to tell if the numbers represent some logical progression or if they are related to a specific event or to a particular royal family. Even more helpful on occasion is the distinctive style that a publisher used to identify an important set or series. Thus, when one sees the Stengel series of royalty from around the world, identification is simplified by the background colors used. The colors remain consistent regardless of who the figure is or what attire they are wearing. Other manufacturers were equally obvious by adding letters to accompany the numbers or by the employing of a standardized sequence pattern.

Coronations and funerals, especially of the British Royal House, are among the themes that are well represented by sets and series of postcards. But this is only the proverbial tip of the iceberg. World War I cartoon types, metamorphics, flag and song cards, coin and stamp cards, in fact about every type and imaginable category of card has had sets and series within it. Swelling the list fur-

ther are the many series that picture the various royal families, one at a time.

Some are informative, some are comical, and others are unusual or historically significant. Imaginative or graphically allegorical, in black and white or in gorgeous color, and not always uniformly remarkable, they share one thing in common: all have been sought, with varying degrees of eagerness and enthusiasm, since their original production. This is the primary reason so many are in evidence today. Even during the "pitch period" of the 1920s, many intrepid souls saved these special cards as keepsakes. This is especially true of British cards (but obviously less so for German and Austrian ones), and accounts for their presence in such vast numbers on the modern market.

To list all the sets and series would be an impossible undertaking. How would anyone know when the list was completed? But there are certain sets and specific series that, because of their beauty or elusiveness, have always excited the minds of collectors. Series and sets deserving special mention are identified here for those who may not be familiar with all of them.

**Tuck's Kings and Queens of England.** Considered by many as one of the best royal sets ever produced. There are three series (614, 615, and 616) of twelve cards each. There is also a fourth series (617) composed of one card (Edward VII) that has been reprinted four times with minor variations. In the first three series, each card features an idealized portrait of the monarch along with a coin of the realm and the royal coat of arms. Either as individuals or as complete sets, they are difficult to locate and are generally priced accordingly.

| Series 614 | Series 615 | Series 616 | Series 617 |
|---|---|---|---|
| William I | Henry IV | Charles I | Edward VII |
| William II | Henry V | Oliver Cromwell | |
| Henry I | Henry VI | Charles II | |
| Stephen | Edward IV | James II | |
| Henry II | Edward V | William and Mary | |
| Richard I | Richard III | Anne | |
| John | Henry VII | George I | |
| Henry III | Henry VIII | George II | |
| Edward I | Edward VI | George III | |
| Edward II | Mary | George IV | |
| Edward III | Elizabeth I | William IV | |
| Richard II | James I | Victoria | |

**Tuck's Queen's Dollhouse.** Not quite as popular but certainly well sought, this set is comprised of a series of six sets of eight cards each (total, 48). They are miniature replicas of English royal residences. Some display an overview of the interiors, while others focus on the furniture groupings. Like the Kings and Queens series, they are not easy to acquire, nor often seen, which adds to their desirability.

**Tuck's Other Series.** The 600 series for coronation of Edward VII also includes cards of family. The 9800 series for the coronation of George V and his family. The 200, 800, 1400, 1900, and 2500 series dealing with Edward VII and his family. The various Oilette series, and earlier numbered series featuring Queen Victoria. Also a 100 series and an 8700 series dealing with royalty other than British.

**F. H. Altman's Rulers of the World.** An untitled set sometimes overlooked, but clearly of more historical merit than either of the Tuck offerings listed above. Copyrighted in 1909, each of the twenty-four cards (664–687) displays an oval picture of a world ruler under the country's flag. Printed at the bottom is the ruler's name and date of ascension, the country's major products and industries, the geographical area, and population—a history lesson in itself. The author highly recommends this series, not only because the cards are so instructive, but also because they are readily available and modestly priced.

**Max Sinz.** A lesser known series of postcards devoted to royalty, this numbered set (25–36), which the author discovered some years ago, is probably an incomplete one. The artist-drawn cards are of good-to-excellent quality and deserve a close look. For the uninformed, the numbers correspond to the following: (25) Wilhelm I; (26) Bismarck; (27) von Moltke (not royalty); (28) Frederick the Great; (29) Napoleon I; (30) Peter the Great; (31) Queen Luise; (32) Maria Theresa; (33) Marie Antoinette;

(34) Maria Stuart; (35) Queen Elizabeth; and (36) Katherine the Great.

**Stengel & Company.** Frequently thought to be the most beautiful and artistically rendered of all royal postcards is the previously mentioned 29,000 series by this Dresden, Germany, company. Portrayed against a deep wine colored background, the various rulers and their spouses are shown in splendid attire with the national symbol (usually a bird) in the upper left-hand corner. Stengel's 29,000 series are beautiful examples of engraving and printing of the highest level.

**Stengel & Company.** Among Stengel's other royal offerings are sets on royal residences, on special events, and on family members. A number of their early cards, which are both beautiful and—alas—elusive, are also highly prized.

**D.R.M.G.** Produced what became known as the national song series (9794). On these, a few notes or words from the national anthem were printed above an inset photograph of the ruler—or ruler and consort—framed in an embossed oval. The predominant colors were usually red, white, and blue although others are known to exist.

**Ottmar Zieher.** Another interesting set of avidly sought items are the stamp cards of Otto Zieher. Referred to by collectors as "O.Z.," Zieher cards have embossed stamp facsimiles and crests of various countries. The royal connection is due to the fact that many of the stamps have images of different monarchs on them. Difficult to obtain, this set, which is believed to number at least forty specimens, would be expensive if purchased complete. Other producers of much wanted stamp cards with a royal connotation are H. Guggenheim, Menke Huber, and G.H.Z.

**H.S.M., M.H.B., and Walter Erhard.** Three publishers renowned for their finely detailed and embossed coin cards. The coin reproductions, which bear likenesses of world rulers, are rendered in beautifully realistic colors. These cards are always popular and continue to be best sellers at shows and auctions.

**Rostro's Massacre of the Monarchs.** This popular artist and caricaturist created what is arguably one of the most difficult of all royal sets to complete. Rostro lampooned every major world monarch of the early twentieth century. Apparently the sets were not saved in great numbers, judging by the fast and furious bidding that ensues every time one is offered for sale. This remarkable series of illustrated social commentary is well worth collecting.

These brief sketches are all too incomplete. Some cursory information regarding a few other well recognized publishers is included to correct, at least in part, some measure of the oversight.

**Rotary.** Among the postcard issues of this internationally acclaimed publisher are these:

| Topic | Numbers |
|---|---|
| Royal Households | 1–100 |
| As above | 1a–100a through— |
| As above | 200a–299a through— |
| As above | 2400a–2499a through— |
| As above | 7100a–7199a through— |
| As above | 7500a–7599a through— |
| As above | 7600a–7699a through— |
| As above | 9400a–9499a |

Included in these series, which are labelled royal households (the author's designation, not Rotary's) are major events like coronations, deaths, marriages, remembrance cards, and sets devoted to royal children.

**Dr. Trenkler and Company.** Enjoys the distinction of being one of the earliest publishers of royal postcards. Trenkler continued to produce material after the beginning of the twentieth century, but it will always be best remembered for its early postcards, especially those of the lesser-known houses of nobility. In this connection, Trenkler's most significant series was the 7000, which was universal in its cast of characters.

**Bas-Relief.** Under this broad umbrella of unusual cards discussed earlier were many publishers. These high relief cards caught the public imagination immediately. Warwick Brothers of Toronto, Taber Bas-Relief, Bamforth, J. Beagles, and Underwood and Underwood were among the publishers. Sometimes the Taber designation was given, sometimes it was not, but most were of uniform manufacture, the exceptions being the few with touches of hand-applied color or speckles. Warwick Brothers published a 100 series; Taber Bas-Relief utilized a 115 Alliance series; Bamforth had a 200 series; Beagles used a 700-numbered series; and Underwood and Underwood did not number theirs. An interesting series published by Philco (600) was called "Portrait Relief" by them.

**J. Beagles.** Long remembered for their real photograph cards of Edwardian actors, actresses, and other notables of the period, Beagles also produced several series of world royalty (real photograph) postcards with numbers that span from 1a to beyond 1,000. Many of these have exceptionally sharp images rivaling the work of modern photographers and are highly prized by collectors.

**Valentines.** Known to countless millions of postcard collectors for their view cards and topicals, Valentines also ventured into the area of royalty. Its offerings included coronation commemoratives, royal family cards, remembrance souvenirs, and cards of royalty in informal attire. Sadly, Valentines did not deem it necessary to number many of its cards, although a few exceptions include a 1300 set and an XL series.

**Photochemie (Berlin).** Sometimes recognized by the symbol Ø (although they did not use it with any degree of consistency), on the most part Photochemie restricted itself to the royal families of Germany. On occasion the company covered some of the Austrian nobility, including a number of cards devoted to the celebration of the sixtieth year of reign of the Emperor Franz Joseph (2000 series). Cards produced for such events as the silver wedding anniversary of Wilhelm II and his twenty-fifth year of reign are especially worthy of merit. Photochemie's main contribution, however, was a continuing series of real photograph cards issued that chronicle the years from 1900 to 1914. Poring over the massive numbers of cards from this publisher (1–3200) is like searching the pages of a family album and watching the changes and events that occurred as time passed. Thanks to Photochemie, the modern collector may purchase prime representations of German social and political history as seen through the eyes and manifested by the deeds of its most exalted citizens.

**B.K.W.I.** Although it is doubtful that the intention was deliberate, this firm produced postcards of some seldom-seen royal figures. Franz Ferdinand, Empress Elisabeth, and Crown Princess Louise are members of this difficult-to-obtain group, and B.K.W.I. counted them, and many more, in its output. Both numbered and unnumbered cards were published, but in neither case was the royal production great in volume. The more well known cards come from the 700 and 800 series of the various royal families (with a strong emphasis on German and Austrian) and the 1–200 series, which is likewise heavily weighted in favor of Teutonic nobility. B.K.W.I. also published an unnumbered black-and-white series of cards picturing activities related to the sixtieth year of Franz Joseph's reign in 1908.

**Gustav Liersch & Co.** Already identified earlier as the largest producer of royal postcards, Liersch cannot go unmentioned in this category. Although its numbering system seems to be a continuous one with infrequently recognized slots for particular kinds of cards, the truth is that all of Liersch's royal material is deserving of at least nominal notice. Much like N.P.G. and Photochemie, their cards would make excellent tools to aid in a reconstruction of German history from the 1890s through the early 1920s. However, Liersch was more intimately connected to the German royal family than either of the other publishers and was able to produce more and varied material. From their early childhood through the first three decades of the twentieth century, Liersch did the children of Germany's emperor proud. In truly biographical style the firm pictured marriages, military careers, family gatherings, recreational activities, offspring announcements—in fact everything—including the daily regimens of the Kaiser's six sons and one daughter. Also part of the large series that continues unabated from number 1 through 8,000 are many other members of German royalty. Some cards are historical, some are enlightening, and all are interesting. It is no overstatement to conclude that the postcards of Gustav Liersch & Company are delight-packed educations in themselves.

## Other Notable Series.

A & G Taylor. Reality series, real photographs

C.W. Faulkner. Series of cards on Edward VII, especially ten-card funeral set. Also George V coronation set

Finke. Series 2500, German royalty

Island Curio Store, Honolulu. Hawaiian royalty

N.D. Photo. Series of various royalty, only some numbered (series 100)

Wrench. Multiple series featuring various royalty and royal residences

B.L. German royalty, 4,000 series

Philco. Various royalty, 3,000 series

LL. George V coronation, 1–100 series; also various royalty and royal residences

A. Papehhin. Royal residences, 1–100 series

Rotophot. Various series (1,000–8,000), mainly German

Weldon's Bazaar of Children's Fashions. A set of six Edward VII souvenir coronation cards for their customers

S.I.P., Paris. Very desirable series of cards of individual rulers. Often embellished with flowers and vines, they are predominantly Real Photo cards that have been numbered

Salmon Series, Warwick Castle Collection. Unnumbered, sepia. Reproductions of paintings of various royalty

A. Leconte, Paris. Numbered series of cards showing royal items located at Versailles, mainly sepia

Manien, Versailles. Historical scenes, items, and royal figures usually related to the pre-1885 period. Mostly in color and numbered.

Central Sales Bureau. This Austrian concessionaire, possibly designated or created by the government, produced two sets of cards (one numbered, one unnumbered) related to the sixtieth year reign of Emperor Franz Joseph. All are real photographs and though originally offered in large numbers they appear to be somewhat scarce now.

## Other Notable Publishers.

Aristophot, Adolph Engel, Axel Eliasson, E.A.S., E.B. & C., Eliotipia Molfese, Tuck's Empire Series, Davidson Brothers, H.C.J. Deeks, and Rotograph.

# 10
# How Rare Is Rare?

One of the most astonishing things about royal post-cards, and the author's primary motive for writing this book, is the amount of erroneous information that surrounds them. In too many instances this misinformation has led well meaning and otherwise knowledgeable dealers to sell common royal postcards at premium prices while placing a lower valuation on truly rare cards whose scarcity is appreciated by only a few advanced collectors.

Conversely, popularity and mass appeal, factors over which most dealers have little control, have frequently taken the place of common sense and research.

It is the aim of this chapter to provide some answers about what is currently available and in what quantity. While putting this book together, I was constantly being brought to a rightful place of humility. And, I might add, of frustration as well. For, try as I might, it became impossible to gather all the necessary information about publishers, sets and series, artists, and the like. Some of these problems created headaches that would severely test the effects of the best prescription drugs, but the fact that the field yet has room for investigation and addition brought a great measure of consolation.

The business of pricing has proved to be a hotly debated area. Valuation is a matter that requires examination. In the first place, pricing is and always has been, a thing apart. As with other collectibles, the relationship between postcard value and postcard scarcity is a difficult knot to unravel. Easier to fathom is the connection between price tag and desirability. Perhaps the problem may be brought into sharper focus by questioning one of the most erroneous of truisms. According to commonly—and mistakenly—held opinion, an item is worth only what someone is willing to pay for it. The conclusion that follows this premise is that the "free market" determines value. Restricted to such items as cabbages and automobile tires, the proposition has cogency. But when the thesis presses itself upon the realm of legitimate antiques and art, it quickly loses validity. Whereas the worth of cabbages and tires, ever-available relative to growth and production, may be determined according to the laws of supply and demand, the values of truly limited articles of merit do not lend themselves to such measurement. As an example, there can be no universally explicable formula that explains why an incomparable masterpiece of art may have value estimates many thousands of dollars apart depending on who is doing the estimating.

The same may be said, although in a decidedly more modest way, for antiques whose numbers are known to be finite. Once they are gone, they are forever gone, and our only reminders of them will be in the form of reproductions. Many royal postcards, whether real photograph, artist-drawn, or other form of printed material, have themselves become "originals," because the paintings or proofs from whence they came were destroyed or lost.

That prices have been added to the rarity scales of the cards herein presented is not intended to be the final word on the matter. Rather it is a concession to convenience and an acknowledgment of the fact that they will continue to be bought and sold. As a cautionary note, the reader should be aware that these prices refer to cards that are free of defects. Tears, delamination, bends, dirt, or stains greatly decrease the selling price and should be considered seriously by those anticipating a purchase.

**A Note about Categories.** Many royal postcards seem to defy attempts to place them in single categories. Some that appear to fit rather nicely under one heading might just as comfortably be placed in another. And, in not a few instances, the Sets and Series category would serve appropriately as a near universal catch-all.

It has been the intention while devising these categories to demonstrate the wondrously rich variety of types into which royalty postcards may be fitted. Conversely, it has not been the author's intention to impose his own system of classification on the collecting world. Clarity and order were the goals and to their realization has every effort been expended.

# Value List of Cards

## Specific Types

| | |
|---|---:|
| Embossed coin cards, R3 | $ 10 |
| Embossed stamp cards, R3–R4 | 10–20 |
| Clay and wax models, R2 | 10 |
| Installment cards, each, R2 | 5–10 |
|     As a set, R5 | 150 |
| Insect cards, all types, R4 | 20 |
| National song cards, R3 | 10 |
| Flag cards | 5 |
| Woven silk, British, R5 | 25 |
| Woven silk, others, R5 | 40–50 |
| Playing cards, R4 | 15 |
| Puzzle cards, R4 | 20 |
| Ruler insets, R2 | 10 |
| Cellophane see-through, R4 | 20 |
| Advertising cards, British, R3–R4 | 10–20 |
| Advertising, Russian, R4 | 20 |
| Advertising, others, R5 | 25 |
| Attachments and add-ons, R2–R4 | 10–15 |
| Bas-relief, British, R2 | 10 |
| Bas-relief, Scandinavian, R2 | 10 |
| Bas-relief, Spanish, R3 | 15 |
| Bas-relief, others, R4 | 20 |
| Fold-outs in packets, R3–R5 | 10–25 |
| Booklets, with detachable cards, R3 | 20 |
| Mechanicals, pre-1900, R5 | 40 |
| Mechanicals, post-1900, R4 | 20 |
| Metamorphics, Napoleon, R4 | 20 |
| Metamorphics, Abdul Hamid, R4 | 20 |
| Metamorphics, others, R5 | 25–40 |
| Fabric patchwork, all cards, R4 | 20 |

## Sets and Series

| | |
|---|---:|
| Tuck, Kings and Queens of England, R3 | 15 |
|     As a series (except 617), R5 | 150 |
| Tuck, Queen's Dollhouses, each, R2 | 5 |
|     As a set, R5 | 200 |
| F.H. Altman, Rulers of the World, R2 | 5 |
|     As a set, R5 | 100 |
| Max Sinz Series, each, R2 | 10 |
|     As a set, R5 | 150 |
| Stengel & Company, 29,000 series, each, R3 | 15 |
|     As a set, R5 | 300 |
| Rostro, Massacre of the Monarchs, each, R4 | 15 |
|     As a set, R5 | 400 |
| L.L., coronation of George V, each, R2 | 5 |
|     As a set, R5 | 50 |
| Tuck, coronation and funeral cards, R2 | 5 |
| Weldon's Bazaar, each, R2 | 5 |
|     As a set, R5 | 40 |
| B.K.W.I., Sixtieth anniversary Franz Joseph, each, R2 | 5 |
|     As a set, R5 | 150 |
| Central Sales Bureau, Sixtieth Anniversary Franz Joseph, each, R3 | 10 |
|     As a set, numbered or unnumbered, R5 | 200 |

## Later Cards of Earlier Motifs

| | |
|---|---:|
| N.D. Series of rulers before 1885, each, R1 | 2 |
| All cards that depict royalty before 1885, each, R1–R2 | 2–10 |
| All cards printed after 1900 that show pre-1900 events or people, R1–R2 | 2–10 |
| Royal residences, R1 | 2–5 |

## Cards by Country

### Abyssinia

| | |
|---|---:|
| All cards, pre-1900, R5 | $ 20–25 |
| All cards, post-1900, R4 | 15 |

### Albania

| | |
|---|---:|
| Wilhelm of Wied, All cards, R5 | 25 |
| Wilhelm's wife and children Pre-1925, R5 | 25–40 |

### Austria-Hungary

| | |
|---|---:|
| **Franz Joseph** | |
| Pre-1900, R3–R4 | 10–20 |
| Formal poses, R2 | 5–10 |
| Informal cards, R3 | 10–15 |
| Military related, R3 | 10–15 |
| Fiftieth Anniversary, R4 | 20 |
| Sixtieth Anniversary, R3 | 10–15 |
| With family members, R3 | 10–15 |
| Artist-drawn, R2–R3 | 10–15 |
| Facsimile signature, R3 | 15 |
| World War I caricatures, R3–R4 | 10–15 |
| Attending special events, R4 | 15–20 |
| Funeral cards, R4 | 20 |
| Memorial cards, R3 | 10–15 |
| **Empress Elisabeth** | |
| All cards, pre-1899, R5 | 25–40 |
| Later reproductions, R1 | 2–5 |
| **Crown Prince Rudolph** | |
| Later cards, R2 | 5–10 |
| **Princess Valerie** | |
| All cards, pre-1900, R4 | 20 |
| All cards, post-1900, R2 | 10 |
| **Franz Ferdinand** | |
| Formal and informal poses, Pre-1900, R4–R5 | 20–40 |
| Post-1900, R3–R4 | 10–20 |
| Assassination-related, R4 | 20 |
| Funeral cards, R4 | 20 |
| Artist-drawn, R4 | 20 |
| With Franz Joseph, R3 | 15 |
| With family, R3–R4 | 15–20 |
| Special occasion, R4 | 20 |
| Facsimile signature, R5 | 30 |
| Cards of children, R4 | 20 |
| **Emperor Carl** | |
| Formal and informal poses Pre-1900, R5 | 25 |
| Post-1900, R3 | 10 |
| Wedding-related, R4 | 20 |
| Coronation, R3–R5 | 15–50 |
| Birth cards of children, R4 | 15–20 |
| Family portraits, R3 | 10–15 |
| Military related, R4 | 20 |
| World War I caricatures, R5 | 35–50 |
| Artist-drawn, R3 | 15 |
| Facsimile signature, R3 | 15 |
| In exile, R5 | 25–40 |
| Death and funeral related, R5 | 25 |
| **Empress Zita** | |
| All cards, pre-1900, R5 | 50 |
| Facsimile signature, R3 | 15 |

Family cards, R2–R3 . . . . . . . . . . . . . . . . . . . . . . $ 10–15
Special occasion, R3–R4 . . . . . . . . . . . . . . . 10–20
With other royalty, R4 . . . . . . . . . . . . . . . . . 15–20
Facsimile signature, R3 . . . . . . . . . . . . . . . 15
Death and funeral cards, R3–R4 . . . . . . . . . . 10–20

Edward VII
All cards, pre-1900, R3–R4 . . . . . . . . . . . . . 10–20
Formal and informal poses, R1–R2 . . . . . . . 5–10
Coronation, R2–R3 . . . . . . . . . . . . . . . . . . . 5–15
Special occasion, R3 . . . . . . . . . . . . . . . . . . 10–15
With other royalty, R3–R4 . . . . . . . . . . . . . . 10–20
Artist-drawn, R2–R3 . . . . . . . . . . . . . . . . . . 10–15
Family cards, R1–R3 . . . . . . . . . . . . . . . . . . 5–15
Military related, R3 . . . . . . . . . . . . . . . . . . . 10–15
Facsimile signature, R3–R4 . . . . . . . . . . . . . 10–20
Caricatures, R4 . . . . . . . . . . . . . . . . . . . . . . 15–20
Death and funeral, R1–R3 . . . . . . . . . . . . . . 5–15

Queen Alexandra
All cards, pre-1900, R3–R4 . . . . . . . . . . . . . 10–20
Formal and informal poses, R2 . . . . . . . . . . . 5–10
With other royalty, R3–R4 . . . . . . . . . . . . . . 10–20
Artist-drawn, R2–R3 . . . . . . . . . . . . . . . . . . 10–15
Facsimile signature, R4 . . . . . . . . . . . . . . . . 15
Death and funeral, R4 . . . . . . . . . . . . . . . . . 15

George V
All cards, pre-1900, R3 . . . . . . . . . . . . . . . . 15
Formal and informal poses, R1–R2 . . . . . . . . 5–10
Coronation, R1–R3 . . . . . . . . . . . . . . . . . . . 5–15
Birth cards of children, R4 . . . . . . . . . . . . . . 15–20
Family cards, R1–R2 . . . . . . . . . . . . . . . . . . 5–10
Artist-drawn, R3 . . . . . . . . . . . . . . . . . . . . . 15
With other royalty, R3 . . . . . . . . . . . . . . . . . 10–15
Military related, R1–R2 . . . . . . . . . . . . . . . . 5–10
Caricatures, R4 . . . . . . . . . . . . . . . . . . . . . . 15–20
Facsimile signature, R3 . . . . . . . . . . . . . . . . 10–15
Special occasion, R3 . . . . . . . . . . . . . . . . . . 10–15

Edward VIII (Prince of Wales)
All cards, pre-1900, R3 . . . . . . . . . . . . . . . . 10–15
Formal and informal poses, R1–R2 . . . . . . . . 5–10
At funeral of Edward VII, R4 . . . . . . . . . . . . 15
Investiture as Prince of Wales, R3 . . . . . . . . . 10–15
School days, R3–R4 . . . . . . . . . . . . . . . . . . 10–20
Pre-World War I visits to France and Germany,
  R4 . . . . . . . . . . . . . . . . . . . . . . . . . . . . . 15–20
World War I related, R3–R4 . . . . . . . . . . . . . 10–20
Touring and state visits as Prince of Wales,
  R3–R4 . . . . . . . . . . . . . . . . . . . . . . . . . . 10–20

George VI
Pre-World War I cards, R3–R4 . . . . . . . . . . . 10–20
World War I related, R4–R5 . . . . . . . . . . . . . 15–25
Marriage related, R3 . . . . . . . . . . . . . . . . . . 10–15

Other British Royalty
All cards, pre-1900, R4 . . . . . . . . . . . . . . . . 15–20
All cards, post-1900, R1–R3 . . . . . . . . . . . . . 5–15

**Germany**
Wilhelm I
Pre-1900 cards, R4–R5 . . . . . . . . . . . . . . . . 20–50
Post-1900 cards, R3–R4 . . . . . . . . . . . . . . . . 10–20
Frederick III
Later cards, R2 . . . . . . . . . . . . . . . . . . . . . . 5–10
Empress Victoria
All cards, pre-1900, R4 . . . . . . . . . . . . . . . . 15–20
Other cards, R4 . . . . . . . . . . . . . . . . . . . . . . 15–20
Wilhelm II
All cards, pre-1900, R4 . . . . . . . . . . . . . . . . 15–20

Formal and informal poses, R1–R2 . . . . . . . . . . . $ 5–10
Military related, R3–R4 . . . . . . . . . . . . . . . . . 10–20
Children's birth, R4 . . . . . . . . . . . . . . . . . . . 15–20
With other royalty, R3–R4 . . . . . . . . . . . . . . 10–20
Caricatures, R2–R4 . . . . . . . . . . . . . . . . . . . 5–20
Special occasion, R4 . . . . . . . . . . . . . . . . . . 15–20
With family, R1–R2 . . . . . . . . . . . . . . . . . . . 5–10
Artist-drawn, R2–R3 . . . . . . . . . . . . . . . . . . 10–15
Facsimile signature, R2–R4 . . . . . . . . . . . . . 10–20
In exile at Doorn, R4 . . . . . . . . . . . . . . . . . . 20

Empress Augusta Victoria
All cards, pre-1900, R4 . . . . . . . . . . . . . . . . 15–20
Formal and informal poses, R2–R3 . . . . . . . . 10–15
Special occasion, R4 . . . . . . . . . . . . . . . . . . 15–20
Artist-drawn, R3–R4 . . . . . . . . . . . . . . . . . . 15–20
Facsimile signature, R2 . . . . . . . . . . . . . . . . 10
In exile, R4 . . . . . . . . . . . . . . . . . . . . . . . . . 15–20
Death and funeral, R4 . . . . . . . . . . . . . . . . . 15–20

Hermine
All cards, R4 . . . . . . . . . . . . . . . . . . . . . . . . 15–20

Crown Prince Wilhelm
All cards, pre-1900, R3–R4 . . . . . . . . . . . . . 10–20
Formal and informal poses, R1–R2 . . . . . . . . 5–10
With family, R1–R2 . . . . . . . . . . . . . . . . . . . 5–10
With other royalty, R3 . . . . . . . . . . . . . . . . . 15
Military related, R2–R3 . . . . . . . . . . . . . . . . 10–15
Caricatures, R4 . . . . . . . . . . . . . . . . . . . . . . 15–20
Births of children, R2 . . . . . . . . . . . . . . . . . 5–10
Marriage, R2–R4 . . . . . . . . . . . . . . . . . . . . . 10–20
Special occasion, R2–R4 . . . . . . . . . . . . . . . 10–20
Facsimile signature, R3 . . . . . . . . . . . . . . . . 10–15
In exile, R4 . . . . . . . . . . . . . . . . . . . . . . . . . 15–20

Other Prussian Royalty
All cards, R2–R4 . . . . . . . . . . . . . . . . . . . . . 10–20

**Germany, Various Royal Houses**
Bavaria
All cards, pre-1900, R5 . . . . . . . . . . . . . . . . 20–40
Anniversary cards, Ludwig II, R3–R4 . . . . . . . 15–20
All cards, Luitpold, post-1900, R3 . . . . . . . . . 10–15
All cards, Ludwig III, post-1900, R3 . . . . . . . . 10–15
All cards, Rupprecht, R2–R4 . . . . . . . . . . . . . 5–20
Other Bavarian royalty, R3–R4 . . . . . . . . . . . 10–20
Saxony
All cards, pre-1900, R5 . . . . . . . . . . . . . . . . 20–50
King Albert, post-1900, R3 . . . . . . . . . . . . . . 10–15
King George, post-1900, R3 . . . . . . . . . . . . . 10–15
King Frederick August, post-1900, R3 . . . . . . . 10–15
Other Saxon royalty, R3–R4 . . . . . . . . . . . . . 10–20
Württemberg
All cards, pre-1900, R5 . . . . . . . . . . . . . . . . 20–50
All cards, post-1900, R4 . . . . . . . . . . . . . . . . 15–30
Other German Royalty
All cards, pre-1900, R5 . . . . . . . . . . . . . . . . 20–50
All cards, post-1900, R3–R5 . . . . . . . . . . . . . 15–25

**Greece**
George I
All cards, pre-1900, R4 . . . . . . . . . . . . . . . . 20
Formal and informal poses, R3 . . . . . . . . . . . 10–15
With family, R3 . . . . . . . . . . . . . . . . . . . . . . 10–15
Artist-drawn, R4 . . . . . . . . . . . . . . . . . . . . . 20
Facsimile signature, R4 . . . . . . . . . . . . . . . . 20
Caricatures, R4 . . . . . . . . . . . . . . . . . . . . . . 20
Special occasion, R4 . . . . . . . . . . . . . . . . . . 20
Military related, R3–R4 . . . . . . . . . . . . . . . . 15–20

| | |
|---|---|
| With other royalty, R4 | $ 20 |
| Assassination related, R4–R5 | 20–30 |
| Funeral cards, R4 | 20 |

Constantine I
| | |
|---|---|
| All cards, pre-1900, R4 | 15–20 |
| Formal and informal poses, R2–R3 | 5–10 |
| Births of children, R3–R4 | 10–15 |
| Marriage, R5 | 25 |
| Coronation, R4 | 20 |
| With family, R2 | 10 |
| Artist-drawn, R4 | 15–20 |
| Military related, R3 | 10–15 |
| Facsimile signature, R4 | 15 |
| Special occasion, R4 | 20 |
| With other royalty, R4 | 20 |

Alexander I
| | |
|---|---|
| All cards, pre-1900, R4 | 15 |
| Formal and informal poses, R2 | 5–10 |
| All other cards, R4 | 15–20 |

George II
| | |
|---|---|
| All cards, pre-1900, R4 | 15 |
| Formal and informal poses, R2 | 5–10 |
| All other cards, R3–R4 | 15–20 |

Other Greek Royalty
| | |
|---|---|
| All cards, R3–R5 | 15–50 |

**Hawaii**
| | |
|---|---|
| All cards, pre-1900, R5 | 25–50 |
| All cards, post-1900, R3–R4 | 10–20 |

**Holland**

William III
| | |
|---|---|
| All cards, pre-1891, R5 | 30–50 |

Dowager Queen Emma
| | |
|---|---|
| All cards, pre-1900, R4–R5 | 20–50 |
| All cards, post-1900, R2–R3 | 10–15 |

Wilhelmina
| | |
|---|---|
| All cards, pre-1900, R4–R5 | 15–35 |
| Formal and informal poses, R1–R2 | 5–10 |
| Coronation, R4 | 20 |
| Marriage, R4 | 20 |
| Birth of Juliana, R2 | 10 |
| Family cards, R1–R2 | 5–10 |
| All other cards, R3 | 10–15 |

Prince Henry
| | |
|---|---|
| All cards, R2–R3 | 5–15 |

Princess Juliana
| | |
|---|---|
| All cards, R2–R3 | 5–15 |

**India (including Afghanistan)**
| | |
|---|---|
| All cards, pre-1900, R5 | 30 |
| All cards, post-1900, R2–R3 | 10–15 |

**Iraq**

Feisal I
| | |
|---|---|
| Installation related, R5 | 35–50 |
| All other cards of Feisal, R5 | 20–35 |

**Italy**

Umberto I
| | |
|---|---|
| All cards, pre-1900, R4 | 15–20 |
| Assassination related, R5 | 20–30 |
| Funeral, R4 | 15–20 |

Queen Margharita
| | |
|---|---|
| All cards, pre-1900, R4 | 20 |
| All cards, post-1900, R3 | 10–15 |

Victor Emmanuel III
| | |
|---|---|
| All cards, pre-1900, R4 | 15–20 |
| Formal and informal poses, R1–R2 | 5–10 |
| Family cards, R1–R2 | 5–10 |
| Births of children, R2–R3 | $ 10–15 |
| Coronation, R4 | 20 |
| Military related, R2–R3 | 5–15 |
| Special occasion, R3 | 15 |
| With other royalty, R4 | 15–20 |
| Artist-drawn, R3–R4 | 10–20 |
| Facsimile signature, R4 | 20 |
| With Mussolini, R4 | 20 |

Queen Elena
| | |
|---|---|
| All cards, pre-1900, R4 | 15–20 |
| Formal and informal poses, R2–R3 | 5–15 |
| All other cards, R2–R3 | 10–15 |

Other Italian Royalty
| | |
|---|---|
| All cards, pre-1900, R4 | 15–20 |
| All cards, post-1900, R2–R3 | 10–15 |

**Japan**

Mutsuhito
| | |
|---|---|
| All cards, pre-1900, R5 | 20–30 |
| Funeral, R5 | 20 |
| All other cards, R3 | 10–15 |

Yoshihito
| | |
|---|---|
| All cards pre-1900, R5 | 15–20 |
| Marriage, R5 | 30 |
| Birth of children, R4 | 15–20 |
| All other cards, R4–R5 | 15–20 |

Hirohito
| | |
|---|---|
| All cards, R4 | 15–20 |

Other Japanese Royalty
| | |
|---|---|
| All cards, R4–R5 | 15–25 |

**Korea**
| | |
|---|---|
| All cards, pre-1900, R5 | 25–100 |
| All cards, post-1900, R4 | 15–20 |

**Liechtenstein**
| | |
|---|---|
| All cards, pre-1900, R5 | 20–50 |
| All cards, post-1900, R4–R5 | 15–40 |

**Luxembourg**

Adolphe
| | |
|---|---|
| All cards, pre-1900, R5 | 25–50 |
| Formal and informal poses, R5 | 20–30 |
| Funeral cards, R5 | 20 |
| All other cards, R4–R5 | 20–50 |

William IV
| | |
|---|---|
| All cards, pre-1900, R5 | 20–50 |
| Marriage, R5 | 50 |
| Coronation, R5 | 25 |
| Formal and informal poses, R4 | 15–20 |
| Births of children, R5 | 20–30 |
| With family, R4–R5 | 15–25 |
| Funeral, R4 | 20 |
| All other cards, R4–R5 | 20–30 |

Maria-Anna
| | |
|---|---|
| All cards, pre-1900, R5 | 20–75 |
| All cards, post-1900, R4 | 20 |

Marie Adelaide
| | |
|---|---|
| All cards, pre-1900, R4 | 15–20 |
| Formal and informal poses, R3–R4 | 15–20 |
| With sisters, R4 | 15–20 |
| Coronation, R5 | 35 |
| In exile, R4–R5 | 20–50 |
| Death and funeral, R5 | 25 |
| All other cards, R4–R5 | 15–30 |

Charlotte
| | |
|---|---|
| All cards, pre-1900, R4 | 15–20 |
| Coronation, R5 | 35 |
| With sisters, R4 | 15–20 |
| Marriage, R5 | 40 |

With family, R4 . . . . . . . . . . . . . . . . . . . . . . . $ 15–20
With other royalty, R4–R5 . . . . . . . . . . . . . . . . 20–30
All other cards, R4–R5 . . . . . . . . . . . . . . . . . . 15–30
All Other Luxembourg Royalty
    All cards, pre-1900, R5 . . . . . . . . . . . . . . . . 20–30
    All cards, post-1900, R4–R5 . . . . . . . . . . . . 15–40

## Monaco
    All cards, pre-1900, R5 . . . . . . . . . . . . . . . . . 25–40
    All cards, post-1900, R4 . . . . . . . . . . . . . . . . 15–20

## Montenegro
Nicholas II
    All cards, pre-1900, R5 . . . . . . . . . . . . . . . . . 20–30
    Formal and informal poses, R3–R4 . . . . . . . . . . 10–20
    With other royalty, R4 . . . . . . . . . . . . . . . . . 20
    Family cards, R3–R4 . . . . . . . . . . . . . . . . . . 15–20
    Special occasion, R5 . . . . . . . . . . . . . . . . . . 30
    Artist-drawn, R4 . . . . . . . . . . . . . . . . . . . . 20
    Caricatures, R5 . . . . . . . . . . . . . . . . . . . . . 30
    Military related, R4–R5 . . . . . . . . . . . . . . . . 15–30
    Facsimile signature, R5 . . . . . . . . . . . . . . . . 30
Prince Danilo
    All cards, R3–R4 . . . . . . . . . . . . . . . . . . . . 10–20
Other Montenegrin Royalty
    All cards, R4–R5 . . . . . . . . . . . . . . . . . . . . 20–40

## Morocco
Muley Hassan
    All cards, pre-1900, R5 . . . . . . . . . . . . . . . . . 50–100
Abdul Aziz
    All cards, pre-1900, R5 . . . . . . . . . . . . . . . . . 20–30
    All cards, post-1900, R4 . . . . . . . . . . . . . . . . 15–20
Yusuf (Mohammed V)
    All cards, pre-1900, R5 . . . . . . . . . . . . . . . . . 20–30
    All cards, post-1900, R4 . . . . . . . . . . . . . . . . 15–20

## Norway
Haakon V
    All cards, pre-1900, R4 . . . . . . . . . . . . . . . . . 15–20
    Formal and informal poses, R1–R2 . . . . . . . . . . 5–10
    Coronation, R4 . . . . . . . . . . . . . . . . . . . . . 15
    Marriage, R5 . . . . . . . . . . . . . . . . . . . . . . 50
    Birth cards, R5 . . . . . . . . . . . . . . . . . . . . . 25
    With other royalty, R3 . . . . . . . . . . . . . . . . . 10–15
    With family, R1–R2 . . . . . . . . . . . . . . . . . . 5–10
    All other cards, R2–R3 . . . . . . . . . . . . . . . . 10–15
Other Norwegian Royalty
    All cards, pre-1900, R5 . . . . . . . . . . . . . . . . 20–30
    All cards, post-1900, R2–R3 . . . . . . . . . . . . . 10–15

## Persia
Mazaffareddin
    All cards, pre-1900, R5 . . . . . . . . . . . . . . . . . 30
    Funeral, R5 . . . . . . . . . . . . . . . . . . . . . . . 25
    All other cards, R4 . . . . . . . . . . . . . . . . . . . 15–20
Mohammed Alim
    All cards, 1900, R5 . . . . . . . . . . . . . . . . . . . 30
    Coronation, R5 . . . . . . . . . . . . . . . . . . . . . 25
    All other cards, R4–R5 . . . . . . . . . . . . . . . . 15–30
Ahmed Mirza
    All cards, pre-1900, R5 . . . . . . . . . . . . . . . . . 20–30
    Coronation, R5 . . . . . . . . . . . . . . . . . . . . . 25
    All other cards, R4–R5 . . . . . . . . . . . . . . . . 15–30

## Portugal
Carlos I
    All cards, pre-1900, R5 . . . . . . . . . . . . . . . . . 20–50
    Formal and informal poses, R2–R4 . . . . . . . . . . 10–20
    Birth of children, R5 . . . . . . . . . . . . . . . . . . 25

With family, R4 . . . . . . . . . . . . . . . . . . . . . . . $ 15
With other royalty, R5 . . . . . . . . . . . . . . . . . . 20–50
Assassination related, R5 . . . . . . . . . . . . . . . . 30
Funeral, R4 . . . . . . . . . . . . . . . . . . . . . . . . 20
Queen Amelia
    All cards, pre-1900, R5 . . . . . . . . . . . . . . . . 20–50
    All cards, post-1900, R3 . . . . . . . . . . . . . . . . 10–15
Manuel II
    All cards, pre-1900, R4 . . . . . . . . . . . . . . . . 15–20
    Formal and informal poses, R2–R3 . . . . . . . . . . 10–15
    Coronation, R3 . . . . . . . . . . . . . . . . . . . . . 15
    Marriage, R4 . . . . . . . . . . . . . . . . . . . . . . 15–20
    All other cards, R4 . . . . . . . . . . . . . . . . . . . 15–20
Other Portuguese Royalty
    All cards, R4 . . . . . . . . . . . . . . . . . . . . . . 15–20

## Rumania
Carol I
    All cards, pre-1900, R5 . . . . . . . . . . . . . . . . . 20–30
    All other cards, R4–R5 . . . . . . . . . . . . . . . . 15–20
Ferdinand
    All cards, pre-1900, R4–R5 . . . . . . . . . . . . . . 15–35
    Formal and informal poses, R3 . . . . . . . . . . . . 10–15
    Military related, R3–R4 . . . . . . . . . . . . . . . . 10–20
    Coronation related, R5 . . . . . . . . . . . . . . . . 35
    With other royalty, R4 . . . . . . . . . . . . . . . . . 15–20
    Births of children, R3 . . . . . . . . . . . . . . . . . 15
    With family, R3 . . . . . . . . . . . . . . . . . . . . . 15
    All other cards, R4 . . . . . . . . . . . . . . . . . . . 15–20
Other Rumanian Royalty
    All cards, R4–R5 . . . . . . . . . . . . . . . . . . . . 15–30

## Russia
Alexander III
    All cards, R5 . . . . . . . . . . . . . . . . . . . . . . 30–75
Empress Dagmar
    All cards, pre-1900, R5 . . . . . . . . . . . . . . . . 25–50
    All cards, post-1900, R4 . . . . . . . . . . . . . . . . 15–20
Nicholas II
    All cards, pre-1900, R5 . . . . . . . . . . . . . . . . 20–35
    Formal and informal poses, R3–R4 . . . . . . . . . . 10–20
    Births of children, R4 . . . . . . . . . . . . . . . . . 15–20
    With other royalty, R3–R5 . . . . . . . . . . . . . . 15–30
    Special occasion, R4 . . . . . . . . . . . . . . . . . . 20
    Artist-drawn, R4 . . . . . . . . . . . . . . . . . . . . 15–20
    Facsimile signature, R4 . . . . . . . . . . . . . . . . 20
    Military related, R4 . . . . . . . . . . . . . . . . . . 15–20
    In exile, R5 . . . . . . . . . . . . . . . . . . . . . . . 25–50
    Assassination related, R5 . . . . . . . . . . . . . . . 25–50
    With Rasputin, R5 . . . . . . . . . . . . . . . . . . . 50
    Caricatures, R4–R5 . . . . . . . . . . . . . . . . . . 20–30
Empress Alexandra
    All cards, pre-1900, R5 . . . . . . . . . . . . . . . . 20–35
    Formal and informal poses, R4 . . . . . . . . . . . . 15–20
    With other royalty, R5 . . . . . . . . . . . . . . . . . 25
    With Rasputin, R4–R5 . . . . . . . . . . . . . . . . 20–30
    All other cards, R4–R5 . . . . . . . . . . . . . . . . 15–30
Royal Children
    All together, R4 . . . . . . . . . . . . . . . . . . . . 15–20
    Only girls, R3–R4 . . . . . . . . . . . . . . . . . . . 10–20
    Alexis only, R4–R5 . . . . . . . . . . . . . . . . . . 20–35
Other Russian Royalty
    All cards, R4–R5 . . . . . . . . . . . . . . . . . . . . 15–30

## Serbia
Milan
    All cards, pre-1900, R5 . . . . . . . . . . . . . . . . 20–35
    All other cards, R4 . . . . . . . . . . . . . . . . . . . 15–20
Natalie
    All cards, R5 . . . . . . . . . . . . . . . . . . . . . . 20–35

Alexander
All cards, pre-1900, R5 . . . . . . . . . . . . . . . . . . . . $ 25–50
Formal and informal poses, R4 . . . . . . . . . . . . . 20
Marriage, R5 . . . . . . . . . . . . . . . . . . . . . . . . . . 30
Assassination related, R5 . . . . . . . . . . . . . . . . 30–50
All other cards, R4–R5 . . . . . . . . . . . . . . . . . . 20–30
Dragin Masin
All cards, R5 . . . . . . . . . . . . . . . . . . . . . . . . . . 25–50
Peter I
All cards, pre-1900, R5 . . . . . . . . . . . . . . . . . . 20–30
Formal and informal poses, R3 . . . . . . . . . . . . . 10–15
With family, R4 . . . . . . . . . . . . . . . . . . . . . . . . 15–20
All other cards, R5 . . . . . . . . . . . . . . . . . . . . . 20–30
Alexander (Yugoslavia)
All cards, pre-1900, R5 . . . . . . . . . . . . . . . . . . 30
All cards, post-1900, R5 . . . . . . . . . . . . . . . . . 20–30
Other Serbian, Yugoslavian Royalty
All cards, R4–R5 . . . . . . . . . . . . . . . . . . . . . . . 15–30

**Siam (Thailand)**
Chulalongkorn
All cards, pre-1900, R5 . . . . . . . . . . . . . . . . . . 20
Formal and informal poses, R4 . . . . . . . . . . . . . 15–20
All other cards, R4–R5 . . . . . . . . . . . . . . . . . . 15–25
Other Siamese Royalty
All cards, R4–R5 . . . . . . . . . . . . . . . . . . . . . . . 15–30

**Spain**
Isabella II
All cards, pre-1900, R5 . . . . . . . . . . . . . . . . . . 30–50
All cards, post-1900, R4–R5 . . . . . . . . . . . . . . . 20–30
Alphonso XIII
All cards, pre-1900, R4–R5 . . . . . . . . . . . . . . . 15–30
Formal and informal poses, R1–R3 . . . . . . . . . . 5–15
Coronation, R4 . . . . . . . . . . . . . . . . . . . . . . . . 15–20
Marriage, R3–R4 . . . . . . . . . . . . . . . . . . . . . . . 15–20
Children's births, R3 . . . . . . . . . . . . . . . . . . . . 10–15
With family, R1–R2 . . . . . . . . . . . . . . . . . . . . . 5–10
With other royalty, R3–R4 . . . . . . . . . . . . . . . . 15–20
Artist-drawn, R4 . . . . . . . . . . . . . . . . . . . . . . . 15–20
Facsimile signature, R4 . . . . . . . . . . . . . . . . . . 20
Caricatures, R4–R5 . . . . . . . . . . . . . . . . . . . . . 15–30
Special occasions, R4 . . . . . . . . . . . . . . . . . . . 15–20
Queen "Ena"
All cards, pre-1900, R4–R5 . . . . . . . . . . . . . . . 15–20
Formal and informal poses, R2 . . . . . . . . . . . . . 5–10
With family, R2 . . . . . . . . . . . . . . . . . . . . . . . . 5–10
All other cards, R3–R4 . . . . . . . . . . . . . . . . . . 10–20

Other Spanish Royalty
All cards, pre-1900, R5 . . . . . . . . . . . . . . . . . . $ 20–30
All cards, post-1900, R4 . . . . . . . . . . . . . . . . . 15–20

**Sweden**
Oscar II
All cards, pre-1900, R5 . . . . . . . . . . . . . . . . . . 20–35
Formal and informal poses, R2–R3 . . . . . . . . . . 5–15
Artist-drawn, R4 . . . . . . . . . . . . . . . . . . . . . . . 15–20
Facsimile signature, R3 . . . . . . . . . . . . . . . . . . 15
With family, R2 . . . . . . . . . . . . . . . . . . . . . . . . 10
With other royalty, R3–R4 . . . . . . . . . . . . . . . . 10–20
Military related, R3 . . . . . . . . . . . . . . . . . . . . . 10–15
Special occasion, R3 . . . . . . . . . . . . . . . . . . . . 10–15
Caricatures, R4 . . . . . . . . . . . . . . . . . . . . . . . . 20
Death and funeral, R4 . . . . . . . . . . . . . . . . . . . 15–20
Gustav V
All cards, pre-1900, R4–R5 . . . . . . . . . . . . . . . 15–25
Formal and informal poses, R2 . . . . . . . . . . . . . 5–10
Marriage, R4 . . . . . . . . . . . . . . . . . . . . . . . . . . 15–20
Coronation, R4 . . . . . . . . . . . . . . . . . . . . . . . . 15–20
With family, R1–R2 . . . . . . . . . . . . . . . . . . . . . 5–10
Children's births, R4 . . . . . . . . . . . . . . . . . . . . 15–20
With other royalty, R3–R4 . . . . . . . . . . . . . . . . 10–20
Special occasion, R3 . . . . . . . . . . . . . . . . . . . . 10–15
Artist-drawn, R3–R4 . . . . . . . . . . . . . . . . . . . . 10–20
Facsimile signature, R3 . . . . . . . . . . . . . . . . . . 10–15
Military related, R3 . . . . . . . . . . . . . . . . . . . . . 10–15
Other Swedish Royalty
All cards, pre-1900, R4–R5 . . . . . . . . . . . . . . . 15–25
All cards, post-1900, R3–R4 . . . . . . . . . . . . . . . 10–15

**Turkey**
Abdul Hamid
All cards, pre-1900, R5 . . . . . . . . . . . . . . . . . . 20–35
All cards, post-1900, R3–R4 . . . . . . . . . . . . . . . 10–20
Mohammed V
All cards, pre-1900, R5 . . . . . . . . . . . . . . . . . . 20–50
All cards, post-1900, R4 . . . . . . . . . . . . . . . . . 15–20
Mohammed VI
Coronation related, R4 . . . . . . . . . . . . . . . . . . 15
Expulsion related, R5 . . . . . . . . . . . . . . . . . . . 25
All other cards, R4–R5 . . . . . . . . . . . . . . . . . . 15–30

**Zanzibar**
All cards, pre-1900, R5 . . . . . . . . . . . . . . . . . . 30–50
All cards, post-1900, R4 . . . . . . . . . . . . . . . . . 15–20